Gayatri Chakravorty Spivak: Live Theory

Also available from the series:

Gayatri Chakravorty Spivak: Live Theory

Mark Sanders

continuum

Continuum International Publishing Group
The Tower Building   80 Maiden Lane
11 York Road   Suite 704
London   New York, NY 10038
SE1 7NX

British Library Cataloguing-in-Publication Data
A catalogue record for this book is available from the British Library.

ISBN: 0-8264-6318-5 (hardback)   0-8264-6319-3 (paperback)

Library of Congress Cataloging-in-Publication Data
A catalog record for this book is available from the Library of Congress.

Typeset by RefineCatch Limited, Bungay, Suffolk
Printed and bound in Great Britain by MPG Books Ltd, Cornwall

For Ginny
Virginia Lieson Brereton
(1944–2004)
Friend and climbing partner

Contents

Acknowledgments

First and foremost my gratitude goes to Gayatri Chakravorty Spivak, who, when I was most in need, offered me her friendship and wise counsel. Although I had been a student in her graduate seminar on Marx for half a semester at Columbia University in the spring of 1992, she really became my teacher when she agreed to direct my PhD dissertation – without my having asked, she took me on as a teaching assistant and mentored me in my teaching. This connection makes it special for me to write about her work in a series aimed in the first place at the student reader.

My first encounter with Spivak's writings was as an English Honours student at the University of Cape Town in 1990. Writing my Honours thesis on Derrida's *Glas*, I discovered '*Glas*-Piece: A *compte rendu*' and 'Displacement and the Discourse of Woman', her meticulous and incisive commentaries on Derrida's difficult book. My engagement with Spivak's work in its own right, however, began at UCT the following year, when, for a module on feminist theory taken for the MA in Literary Studies, Dorothy Driver distributed a photocopy pack of seven of Spivak's essays. The first of the photocopied texts was 'Can the Subaltern Speak?' To the disbelief of my own students, this document, now much annotated, worn and torn, is the copy of the essay that I continue to use when I teach. A memento of a time when none of us could afford to buy the books – I still also have my photocopies of *Glas*, *Margins of Philosophy* and other works by Derrida – it also reminds me of my debt to another dedicated and demanding teacher.

In writing this book, I was greatly helped by the responses and insights of students in my Postcolonial Theory seminar at Brandeis University in the spring of 2005 – in particular, Yishan Lam, Elisa Harkness and Laura John. They demanded clarity and, on occasion, endeavoured to provide it when I could not.

My thanks go to Dina Al-Kassim for inviting me to speak as part of a panel on Spivak's *A Critique of Postcolonial Reason* at the International Association for Philosophy and Literature conference at Stony Brook, New York, in May 2000, which afforded me an opportunity to develop the thinking that has gone into this book. My paper from that panel, which forms part of Chapter 3, appeared in *Interventions: The International Journal of Postcolonial Studies* (4.2 [2002]), and is reprinted by permission of Taylor & Francis Ltd (http://www.tandf.co.uk). A portion of Chapter 1 appeared in a different form in *Postmodern Culture* (10.1 [1999]); it is reprinted by kind permission of the editors.

I am most grateful to Jeanie Tietjen for her research assistance, her attention to detail in locating and assembling the many, widely scattered, pieces of Spivak's oeuvre that I needed to read for this study.

Melanie Micir was always helpful in liaising between me and Gayatri – who warmly supported this project from the beginning and was always forthcoming with information when I requested it.

As always, I thank Louise Kuhn for being there, watching over me while I wrote another book.

New York City, Summer 2005

Abbreviations

The following abbreviations have been employed for frequently cited works by Spivak:

CPR   *A Critique of Postcolonial Reason: Toward a History of the Vanishing Present*

CSS   'Can the Subaltern Speak?'

IOW   *In Other Worlds: Essays in Cultural Politics*

OTM   *Outside in the Teaching Machine*

Chapter 1

Literature, Reading and Transnational Literacy

> Without the reading of the world as a book, there is no
> prediction, no planning, no taxes, no laws, no welfare, no war.
> Yet . . . leaders read the world in terms of rationality and
> averages, as if it were a textbook. The world actually writes
> itself with the many-leveled, unfixable intricacy and openness
> of a work of literature.
> – 'Reading the World: Literary Studies in the Eighties'

How might responsibility in today's world be understood by the literary reader? Can training in a literary habit of reading give a special character to ethical and political responsibility? Can reading, in any sense of the word, lead to a responsible global literacy? These are questions that Gayatri Chakravorty Spivak has posed, with ever-increasing urgency, for many years. The world that she questions is the one being remade by globalization and to some extent still coming to terms with an older legacy not only encompassing colonization but also the social formations preexisting it – which typically have a particularly profound impact on the position of women. Signs of Spivak's singular contribution to a thinking of responsibility, of her opening of the study of literature in the narrow sense to an audacious crossing of disciplines, these questions are, accordingly, also the ones that will inform this book.[1]

Reading the world as one would read a book is a classic topos for the mind directed outward. In one of its most famous elaborations, by René Descartes in *Discourse on the Method of Properly Conducting One's Reason and of Seeking the Truth in the Sciences* (1637), the topos suggests the course of a mind of a pupil gaining its independence: 'as soon as I reached an age which allowed me to emerge from the tutelage of my teachers, I abandoned the study of letters altogether, and resolving to study no other science than that which I could find within myself or else in the great book of the world, I spent the rest of my youth in travelling' (33). In

Spivak, as in Descartes, it is the student who is the protagonist of a passage toward intellectual maturity as a going-out into the world. He or she is the subject not of travelling in the conventional sense but of what Spivak terms 'transnational literacy', the ability to read the world in its differences even when received categories such as 'literature' or 'decolonization' impose a uniformity – and, before long, an evaluation of what is less and what is more, what worse and what better.

In 'Teaching for the Times' (1995), Spivak addresses the economic migrant to the United States who cannot not hope for justice under capitalism, but who, because of this hope, one that is always disavowed, may tend too readily to identify his or her experience with that of other diasporic groups and with that of citizens in their decolonized countries of origin. The migrant group is the source of future teachers (whom Spivak encounters in the classroom as graduate students), who want to change the capitalist system for the better. The tendency of migrants to the United States has been to subscribe unquestioningly to liberal multiculturalism and to conduct an oppositional identity politics based on national origin, or to undertake a politics of solidarity on the assumption of a shared 'post-colonial' history. It is to them that Spivak commends and explains transnational literacy:

> Learning this praxis, which may produce interruptions to capitalism from within, requires us to make future educators in the humanities transnationally literate, so that they can distinguish between the varieties of decolonization on the agenda, rather than collapse them as 'post-coloniality.' I am speaking of transnational *literacy*. We must remember that to achieve literacy in a language is not to become an expert in it. . . . Literacy produces the skill to differentiate between letters, so that an articulated script can be read, reread, written, rewritten. . . . It allows us to sense that the other is not just a 'voice,' but that others produce articulated texts, even as they, like us, are written in and by a text not of our own making. It is through transnational literacy that we can invent grounds for an interruptive praxis from within our disavowed hope in justice under capitalism. ('Teaching for the Times' 193–4)

The context for Spivak's appeal for transnational literacy in 'Teaching for the Times' is the observation, easily made by literary critics, that certain sectors of the decolonized world have not produced the 'spectacular experimental fiction' of, say, Indian writing in English.[2] In order to explain this phenomenon, instead of making it an excuse for dismissal, Spivak calls for 'a disarticulating rather than a comparative point of view'. Bangladesh becomes her national example: 'You will hardly ever find an entry from Bangladesh on a course on postcolonial or Third World literature. Bangladesh is stylistically non-competitive on the international market' ('Teaching for the Times' 194). In the case of Bangladesh, the market to which Spivak refers is not only the world book market, but also the one mapped by global capital, and in which gender is a prominent faultline: 'The UN has written it off as the lowest on its list of developing countries, its women at the lowest rung of development' ('Teaching for the Times' 194). Spivak outlines a series of relevant differences of which students of literature ought to be aware but, typically, are not:

> Our students will not know that, as a result of decolonization from the British in 1947, and liberation from West Pakistan in 1971, Bangladesh had to go through a double decolonization; that as a result of the appropriation of its language by the primarily Hindu Bengali nationalists in the nineteenth century, and the adherence of upper-class Bangladeshis to Arabic and Urdu, the Bangladeshis have to win back their language inch by inch. . . . [And] because of the timing and manner of Bangladesh's liberation, the country fell into the clutches of the transnational global economy in a way significantly different from the situation both of the Asian-Pacific *and* the older postcolonial countries. The transnationally illiterate student might not know that the worst victim of the play of the multinational pharmaceuticals in the name of population control is the woman's body; that in the name of development, international monetary organizations are substituting the impersonal and incomprehensible State for the older more recognizable enemies-cum-protectors: the patriarchal family. ('Teaching for the Times' 194)

In short, Spivak demands of the student of modern languages and literatures a thoroughgoing interdisciplinarity. Only by reading outside of literature as a narrowly conceived discipline can the student hope to tease out the kind of historical, political, economic, religious and linguistic differences (for the sake of brief illustration I elide a number of them) that Spivak outlines.[3] Learning to discern such differences will, in effect, lead the student toward a questioning of 'literature' in the narrow sense as the dominant category. Having overcome, as did Descartes, the control exercised over his or her mind by 'letters', he or she may ultimately gain an independence from 'literature' as a received disciplinary category that forestalls 'the reading of the world as a book' in the manner advocated by Spivak in the passage I quote as my epigraph (*IOW* 95). Confronted with the case of Bangladesh, the student will realize that 'the most dynamic minds are engaged in alternative development work, not literary production' ('Teaching for the Times' 194). This apparently very minor realization is important, less for the (to be sure, highly speculative) thesis that it contains about Bangladeshi literary history, than for the de-centring of literary studies as a privileged site for interpreting the human condition.

Does this mean that transnational literacy is unrelated to the literary method of reading in which literary studies specializes? Is it simply about interdisciplinarity at the level of information-retrieval? 'On the contrary,' Spivak writes, 'we expand the definition of literature to include social inscription' ('Teaching for the Times' 195). Unlike the youthful Descartes, Spivak's student will not abandon the study of letters. Indeed, the literary will always have been Spivak's point of departure and her constant point of reference. The idea that transnational literacy 'allows us to sense that the other is not just a "voice," but that others produce articulated texts, even as they, like us, are written in and by a text not of our own making' ('Teaching for the Times' 193) is a clue to the relationship between it and a literary method of reading as training for a relation of ethical singularity with the other. Reading is thus related to responsibility. There is, moreover, something literary about displacing literature in the narrow sense. The course of Spivak's life and work may be described in terms of this displacement.

Life and work

Born in 1942 in Calcutta in Bengal, then part of British India, Gayatri Chakravorty Spivak belongs to the generation immediately preceding the one that Salman Rushdie called 'midnight's children' – those born at the stroke of Indian independence in 1947.[4] The daughter of middle-class 'ecumenical, secularist, protofeminist, "philosophical Hindu" parents' ('Lives' 211), she attended a missionary school, where her teachers were tribal Christians. She enrolled at Presidency College at the University of Calcutta in 1955, graduating first in First Class with Honours in English in 1959. Borrowing money, she travelled to the United States in 1961 to enter the graduate programme in English at Cornell University in Ithaca, New York. In 1962 she shifted, 'for financial reasons' ('Lives' 211), to Comparative Literature. She was 'the first woman to hold a lodging scholarship at intellectually arrogant Telluride House' ('Lives' 211), where her fellow residents at the time included Paul Wolfowitz, the neoconservative who became United States Deputy Secretary of Defense under George W. Bush, and presently heads the World Bank.

At Cornell Spivak studied under Paul de Man, writing a dissertation on the poetry of William Butler Yeats, and received her PhD in 1967. In 1965 she joined the Department of Comparative Literature at the University of Iowa as an Assistant Professor. The department had been founded in the 1940s by René Wellek, one of the European émigrés who introduced Comparative Literature as a discipline to the United States academy. While at Iowa she came across an entry in the Minuit catalogue for *De la grammatologie*, ordering it 'because it looked interesting' ('Foreword: Upon Reading' xix). Until then she had never heard of Jacques Derrida, nor had she been aware of the landmark 1966 Johns Hopkins University Conference on the Structuralist Controversy that he had addressed along with Jacques Lacan and other French thinkers. So struck was Spivak on reading *De la grammatologie* that she decided to translate it, entering into a contract for the translation and a long preface with the University of Massachusetts Press 'in 1967 or 1968' – it was later taken to Johns Hopkins University Press by J. Hillis Miller, who 'had already started organizing Derrida's U.S. career' ('Thinking about Edward Said' 519).

Spivak's decision to translate *De la grammatologie* would radically change the course of her career; it is with some understatement that, in a 1989 interview, she describes herself as 'a modernist who has stumbled into deconstruction . . . who did some deconstruction on her own in a certain way, and has stuck with it because it has lasted her in the wash' ('Naming Gayatri Spivak' 84). After publishing a monograph for young adults entitled *Myself Must I Remake: The Life and Poetry of W.B. Yeats* (1974), her translation *Of Grammatology* appeared in 1976 along with her influential translator's preface. Within a few years, she was an active participant in debates on 'post-structuralism', and was defining herself in critical relation to French feminist theory (Cixous, Kristeva, Irigaray), which had begun to influence American feminist literary scholars in the 1970s, and was developing a feminist critique of Derrida. At the same time, she began translating the fiction of Bengali author Mahasweta Devi, the story 'Draupadi' appearing in the journal *Critical Inquiry* in 1981. A constant commentator on new work by Derrida (most notably *Glas*, *La carte postale*, *Éperons/Spurs*), her deconstructive re-readings of Karl Marx began to appear in the early 1980s.

'Can the Subaltern Speak?' (1988), the long essay for which Spivak is perhaps best known, brought all of these strands together. First drafted in 1982–83, it read Marx's *The Eighteenth Brumaire of Louis Bonaparte* deconstructively, employing the resultant critique of 'representation' (shifting imperceptibly, for many thinkers, between cognitive and political senses of the word, and thereby eliding the workings of ideology) to analyse the staging of the *sati* (widow self-immolation) in colonial law as well as in Hindu scripture. Ending with a coda on Bhubaneswari Bhaduri, a distant relative of Spivak who in the 1920s took her own life rather than carry out a political assassination, 'Can the Subaltern Speak?' is the first instalment in a series of meditations by Spivak, up to her most recent work, on the politics of suicide.

Spivak began her close association with the Subaltern Studies group of historians in 1984, and her critical engagement with their reconception of Indian historiography is the subject not only of 'Can the Subaltern Speak?' but also of two of the major essays collected in *In Other Worlds: Essays in Cultural Politics* (1987), which assembled her writings on literature and critical theory, including 'French Feminism in an International Frame' and her reading of Marx in 'Scattered Speculations on the Question of Value', as well as her translations of Devi's 'Draupadi' and 'Breast-Giver'. With Ranajit Guha she coedited *Selected Subaltern Studies* (1988). A collection of interviews entitled *The Post-Colonial Critic: Interviews, Strategies, Dialogues* (1990) brought her work to a wider readership, confirming what 'Can the Subaltern Speak?' and essays such as 'Three Women's Texts and a Critique of Imperialism' (1985) and 'The Rani of Sirmur: An Essay in Reading the Archives' (1985) had already established, namely, her position as a major figure in the nascent field of postcolonial theory – along with Edward Said, whose *Orientalism* (1978) is typically regarded as its founding work, and Homi K. Bhabha, whose essays were collected in *The Location of Culture* (1994).[5] Over time, however, Spivak has declared herself uneasy with the appellation 'postcolonial theorist'.

By the late 1980s Spivak had become not only an academic 'star' in the United States,[6] garnering a series of prestigious university appointments, but also a major international intellectual, highly sought after as a speaker at conferences and other gatherings in culture and the arts all over the world. It was as if her stipulations for 'reading the world' were being realized in her own career. At nearly the same time, she became involved, in ways that she only talked about publicly years later, in teacher training at schools teaching basic literacy to *ādivāsis* or 'tribals' – members of the aboriginal peoples of the subcontinent – in rural Bangladesh and India.[7] Bringing together two dimensions of her lifelong concern with teaching, a literary reading of the world taught in the metropole began to be complemented by an emphasis on literacy in the periphery. 'Righting Wrongs' (2004) and 'Ethics and Politics in Tagore, Coetzee, and Certain Scenes of Teaching', (2002), which I discuss later in this chapter, are the key texts of this departure.

Two of Spivak's books from the 1990s, *Outside in the Teaching Machine* (1993) and *A Critique of Postcolonial Reason: Toward a History of the Vanishing Present* (1999), especially the final chapter of the latter, reflect her frenetic shuttling across the world – and the attempt, as in 'Teaching for the Times,' to develop an awareness of difference within a totality scripted by global capital. Many of the essays in *Outside in the Teaching Machine* are thus occupied with underlining the difference between the position of the metropolitan migrant and the citizen of the decolonized nation-state.[8] Particularly striking is the book's attention to migrant cultural politics in essays on Salman Rushdie's *The Satanic Verses* and Hanif Kureishi's film *Sammy and Rosie Get Laid*. *A Critique of Postcolonial Reason*, combining work done over fifteen years, including 'Can the Subaltern Speak?', endeavours to write a 'history of the vanishing present'.

Spivak's most recent book, *Death of a Discipline* (2003), brought her full circle by addressing the transformation of Comparative Literature as a discipline, specifically through an alliance with Area Studies, a project that she has been practically engaged in at Columbia University over the last several years. Complementing this work's emphasis on a new, global Comparative Literature, and a commitment to local idiomaticity, is her ongoing translation of Mahasweta Devi's fiction. Spivak's English translation of Devi's novel *Chotti Munda and His Arrow* also appeared in 2003. Although she stated the same year that she would never write her memoirs (' "On the Cusp" ' 215), a fragment of a projected memoir appeared in *Critical Inquiry* in 2005 ('Thinking about Edward Said'). Two new books are in the pipeline: *Other Asias* and *Red Thread*. They comprise essays written over the last decade or more.[9] Since their final shape has not been determined, I discuss in detail here *A Critique of Postcolonial Reason*, the book that most fully articulates, in dense and difficult ways that require careful explication, Spivak's ideas about literature, reading and ethics.

A Critique of Postcolonial Reason

> Marx could hold *The Science of Logic* and the Blue Books
> together; but that was still only Europe; and in the doing it
> came undone.
> – *A Critique of Postcolonial Reason*

'As I work at this at the end of a book that has run away from me, I am of course open to your view. You will judge my agenda in the process. . . . You work my agenda out' (*CPR* 357–8). Spivak's *A Critique of Postcolonial Reason* addresses an 'implied reader' several times towards its end, inviting a response (cf. *CPR* 421). We are deep in the ultimate chapter, on Culture, where the 'this' refers to questions of cultural politics. By analogy with Marx, who, envisioning a reader for *Capital*, 'attempted to make the factory workers rethink themselves as agents of production, not as victims of capitalism', Spivak asks her implied readers – hyphenated Americans, economic and political migrants from the decolonized South – to 'rethink themselves as *possible* agents of exploitation, not its victims' (*CPR* 357, cf. 402).[10] The persistent call, voiced in *Outside in the Teaching Machine* and in 'Teaching for the Times', for the migrant to the North to distinguish, in terms of victimage and agency, between him- or, especially, herself and the citizen of the postcolonial nation is reiterated in *A Critique of Postcolonial Reason*. But by the time it includes its implied author and reader in the exhortation, 'let us want a different agency, shift the position a bit' (*CPR* 358, cf. 402), *A Critique of Postcolonial Reason* has given its reader more to work out than an agenda, an itinerary of agency in complicity. It has also blazed an intricate trajectory on what it means to read the present global conjuncture, and to be a reader within it. To interdisciplinary 'transnational literacy' as contemplated in 'Teaching for the Times' is joined a specifically literary theory of reading.

The Native Informant as reading position

The Preface to *A Critique of Postcolonial Reason* places Spivak's theory of reading in an expansive historical context, explaining how the figure that she calls the 'Native Informant' appears and withdraws at successive junctures. Tracking this figure, which changes but never quite disappears, is what shapes the book:

> My aim, to begin with, was to track the figure of the Native

Informant through various practices: philosophy, literature, history, culture. Soon I found that the tracking showed up a colonial subject detaching itself from the Native Informant. After 1989, I began to sense that a certain postcolonial subject had, in turn, been recoding the colonial subject and appropriating the Native Informant's position. Today, with globalization in full swing, telecommunicative informatics taps the Native Informant directly in the name of indigenous knowledge and advances biopiracy. (*CPR* ix)

During the era of colonial rule – Spivak is not specific about location, but India is implied – the provider of information about the locality in question is displaced somewhat by the 'colonial subject'. Spivak associates this figure with those deliberately and more or less willingly assimilated 'interpreters' anticipated by Thomas Babington Macaulay in his 'Minute on Indian Education' (1835): 'a class of persons, Indian in blood and colour, but English in taste, in opinions, in morals, and in intellect' (quoted in *CPR* 268). There is a sense in which this intermediary class cannot quite *inform*; in which it has 'detached' itself from the remainder of the body politic that has not gone through this process of assimilation.

In India, this process continued for more than one hundred years. With the end of the Cold War (1989 was the year the Berlin Wall came down) things changed once again. Spivak does not spell out the factors that led to it. Nevertheless, in a preliminary way, we can discern a context of multiculturalism in the metropole (Great Britain, United States) in which the migrant plays the role of national-cultural broker. This context is the one made clear in 'Teaching for the Times' and *Outside in the Teaching Machine* (see especially *OTM* 255–84). In Spivak's picture the position of the migrant corresponds roughly to that of members of the elite in the country of origin. Because of its genealogy in colonial subject-making that detached it from unmodified nativity and gave it a stake in colonial language, culture and political economy, the postcolonial subject may find itself appropriating a position to which it is not, strictly speaking, entitled; this may result in various forms of nativism. The main thrust of Spivak's *Critique* is directed at this second figure. It is in this respect broadly Kantian: there are limits to what human beings can *know*, to what information we can in good faith supply, and therefore any claim to know, to have information, is to be subjected to a kind of examination called 'critique' – which tests its relation to truth and, in Socratic fashion, exposes the extent of its baselessness and measures its degree of interestedness.[11]

The final instantiation of the Native Informant breaks with the dynamics of mediation – the education and culture of the 'civilizing mission' and aspirations of local and diasporic class mobility. Directly tapping the Native Informant (*tele-* indicates distance), 'informatics' works differently: biochemical formulae, genetic code – these are the elements traded or, through the 'biopiracy' of patenting crops,[12] subject to what David Harvey terms 'accumulation by dispossession' (*The New Imperialism* 137–82). In this scenario, the Native Informant as postcolonial subject is not quite irrelevant. Whether as metropolitan migrant or citizen of the decolonized nation-state, he or she serves as a facilitator for exchange between metropole and nation or transnational corporation and country of origin. It is for this figure that Spivak believes that transnational literacy and the more patient activity of a literary method of reading remain important. This is why Spivak intervenes in the humanities: 'philosophy, history, literature, and culture'.

A question arises: does Spivak's analysis, and her characterization of an implied reader, mean that the lessons of her book are of relevance only to postcolonial national citizens or migrants? She does not give a direct answer to this question in *A Critique of Postcolonial Reason*. I think, however, that it would be wrong to restrict her 'reading position' to citizens of decolonized countries alone.[13] In globalization, as soon as one enters a relation of connectedness in distance (in the mode of *tele-*), one is implicated. Spivak says: be aware of what you are doing, to whatever extent possible, so that, when you aspire to do good, you perceive the limits within which you operate. This is how, in *A Critique of Postcolonial Reason*, the ambit of the first of Kant's three critiques, *Critique of Pure Reason* (1781/1787) – What can I know? – shades into that of the second, *Critique of Practical Reason* (1788): What ought I to do? Responsibility depends not on one's nationality or race, but on one's *position*. Spivak's minute attention to literature and a literary method of reading in *A Critique of Postcolonial Reason* may be read as designed to articulate the scope of Kant's first and second critiques.

In the light of her ideas about ethics, responsibility and reading, it is clear that to track the composite figure Spivak names the Native Informant is not simply to trace and analyse its outlines as it emerges in colonial or postcolonial discourse. This has implications for the rhetorical conduct of the book itself. Finding that the Native Informant reveals, in its trail, a dispropriable 'position', a borrowed one not strictly anyone's own, the tracker herself performs the figure, and is, in turn, performed by it. Giving shape to the tracker, this mimetic tracking engages the trace of the other which sends this book on its way. The writer, in other words, conjures up a reader. The result of figuring, and taking up, the '(im)possible perspective of the Native Informant' is an interventionist writing that is quasi-advocative in its conduct.

Amplifying and deepening Spivak's thinking, *A Critique of Postcolonial Reason* revises major published texts to go with considerable new ones. Arranged into four long chapters – headed 'Philosophy', 'Literature', 'History', 'Culture' – and a small appendix on 'The Setting to Work of Deconstruction', it reframes such well-known essays as 'Can the Subaltern Speak?', 'The Rani of Sirmur', and 'Three Women's Texts and a Critique of Imperialism' so that, in addition to being key interventions in colonial-discourse studies and postcolonial studies, they add to the wider critical idiom by developing insights in ethics and reading gained from a thinking of postcoloniality. Among its surprises is the insistent, and at times cryptic, conversation with the later writings of Paul de Man (to whom *A Critique of Postcolonial Reason* is jointly dedicated) on irony, allegory and parabasis, which Spivak deploys in terms of a disruptive speaking- and reading-otherwise. What emerges is an ethics of reading, of the making of a reader; and, from that, a way for writer and reader to acknowledge and negotiate discursive and socio- and geo-political situatedness as complicity. It eschews simple oppositionality.[14] No position is 'proper' to one side, and all are appropriable by the other: the Native Informant leaves in its tracks a colonial subject turned postcolonial turned agent-instrument of global capital (cf. *CPR* 223 n42). This is the larger itinerary of agency in complicity mapped by *A Critique of Postcolonial Reason*, of which it repeatedly advises its declared implied reader. Of more than equal interest are the book's less overt lineaments.

A Critique of Postcolonial Reason begins by shadowing Immanuel Kant's *Critique of Judgement* (1790) and its foreclosure of the Native Informant. Literary critics usually read the third of Kant's critiques for its account of the beautiful and the sublime. In Spivak's careful reading, however, the aesthetic is strongly linked to the ethical – the subject of Kant's second critique. Both the aesthetic and the ethical are, however, as Spivak shows, connected to an 'anthropology' – a thinking of the human. This lends Kant's philosophical discourse a historicity (or referentiality) that must be covered over in order for it to become a consistent or transcendental discourse of truth. The import of such foreclosure is ethical, and affectively tagged in ways that psychoanalysis allows us to think when it opens the ethical in the dynamics of transference and counter-transference (*CPR* 107, 207). Turning to the psychoanalytic lexicon – *A Critique of Postcolonial Reason* 'sometimes conjure[s] up a lexicon-consulting reader for the new cultural studies' (*CPR* x) – Spivak finds foreclosure set out by Freud and Lacan as a rejection (*Verwerfung*) by the ego of an idea and, along with that idea, the affect connected to it (*CPR* 4). To imagine the (im)possible perspective of the Native Informant in Kant, and in the other 'source texts of European ethico-political selfrepresentation' (*CPR* 9), is thus to respond not only to a failure of representation as a lack of, or limit to, knowledge, but also to a disavowal that is ethical in character.

The main point of using the psychoanalytic concept-metaphor of foreclosure is to register an unacknowledged failure of relation, one amounting to a denial of access to humanity: 'I shall docket the encrypting of the name of the "native informant" *as the name of Man* – a name that carries the inaugurating affect of being human. . . . I think of the "native informant" as a name for that mark of expulsion from the name of Man – a mark crossing out the impossibility of the ethical relation' (*CPR* 5–6). These sentences are, as Spivak frequently is in *A Critique of Postcolonial Reason*, cryptic. Let us decipher: To be a native informant is to speak, after a fashion. The native informant's role in ethnography, Spivak's source for the term, is to provide information, to act as a source and/or an object of knowledge. When this is the function of the native informant, an ethical relation is impossible, for, strictly speaking, the investigator has no responsibility for the informant. It may as well be a *telematic* tapping of genetic material or another subindividual form of appropriation. Yet a ruse is perpetrated that the investigator does have responsibility. In this sense, the ethnographic designation 'native informant' crosses out this impossibility of relation but does not cancel it. Spivak alludes to Jacques Derrida's practice of placing certain concept-words '*sous rature*', under a bold typographic 'X', which in *Of Grammatology* she translates as 'under erasure': 'This is to write a word, cross it out, and then print both word and deletion. (Since the word is inaccurate, it is crossed out. Since it is necessary, it remains legible.)' (Spivak, 'Translator's Preface' xiv). The mode of reading proposed and performed in *A Critique of Postcolonial Reason* strives to preserve an impossibility of responsibility under erasure.

As an alternative to the foreclosure that she discloses, Spivak proposes a 'commitment not only to narrative and counternarrative, but also to the rendering (im)possible of (another) narrative' (*CPR* 6). How are we to explicate this typographic matrix? In order to do so, we have to enter briefly Spivak's dense and difficult reading of the placement of the Native Informant in the *Critique of Judgement*, in which 'he is needed as the example for the heteronomy of the determinant, to set off the autonomy of the reflexive judgment, which allows freedom for the rational will' (*CPR* 6). In the 'Analytic of the Sublime', in the first part of the *Critique*, the terror of a certain 'raw man' stands in, metaleptically, as a precursor to rational subjectivity. That 'raw man' is as yet unnamed. In the 'Critique of Teleological Judgement', the second part of the *Critique*, Kant gives him a name. There the New Hollander (*Neuholländer*, or Australian Aborigine) and the inhabitant of Tierra del Fuego (*Feuerländer*) illustrate how, without making reference to something supersensible – such as the concept 'Man' – one cannot easily decide 'why it is necessary that men should exist'. This, Kant writes in parentheses, is 'a question which is not so easy to answer if we cast our thoughts by chance on the New Hollanders or the inhabitants of Tierra del Fuego' (quoted in *CPR* 26). Kant's Fuegan, according to Spivak, 'is not only not the subject as such; he also does not quite make it as an example of the thing or its species as natural product' (*CPR* 26). Calling her reading of Kant 'mistaken' (*CPR* 9), Spivak deliberately breaks with conventions of philosophy – for which Kant's 'raw man' might be an 'unimportant rhetorical detail' (*CPR* 26) – by figuring, on a minimal empirical basis (little more than the fact they existed), the perspective of the New Hollander or Fuegan.[15] This perspective is (im)possible – bracketing the 'im' puts impossibility under erasure without submitting to the ruse of cancelling it – in that it answers to a call as one would reply, having not actually been asked for an answer, to a rhetorical question.[16]

The Kantian text appears to summon a native informant and his perspective only to guard against their arrival as anything but that which confirms, through ideational and affective – and hence ethico-political – foreclosure, the European as human norm. The Native Informant enjoys 'limited access to being-human' (*CPR* 30). Spivak bets on the name 'native informant' as what encrypts the 'name of Man' and which continues, '[a]s the historical narrative moves from colony to postcolony to globality . . . [to] inhabit . . . us so that we cannot claim the credit of our proper name' (*CPR* 111). With this self-implicating history of the present, the double task of the reader is at once to bind herself to the possibility of the Native Informant's perspective as a narrative perspective (*CPR* 9), and to dramatize its foreclosure by resisting the ruse of simply cancelling its impossibility. Let us bring this home: Identitarianism within multiculturalism, for instance, is, when it verges on nativism, a species of self-deception, of disavowal of one's structural position within global capitalism. As I have suggested, one's position is not necessarily restricted by one's national origin, race, or other marker of 'identity'. Here the reader's double task is taken up typographically by bracketing the negative 'im-'. Elsewhere in *A Critique of Postcolonial Reason*, Spivak employs other rhetorical strategies.

In Spivak's reading of Kant, and in her reading of Hegel which follows it, typographics give way to prosopopoeia – '[a] rhetorical figure by which an imaginary or absent person is represented as speaking or acting' (*OED*). Weaving her text from loose ends of the empirical and the philosophical, Spivak imagines, from the trace of the unacknowledged foreclosure of their perspective, the New Hollander and the Fuegan as 'subject[s] of speech'. In order to operate them as perspectives of narrative, a rhetoric of prosopopoeia, which necessarily involves a counterfactual 'if', is the minimally requisite strategy for entering an affective vein, and hence for opening the possibility of an ethical relation:

> But if in Kant's world the New Hollander . . . or the man from Tierra del Fuego could have been endowed with speech (turned into the subject of speech), he might well have maintained that, this innocent but unavoidable and, indeed, crucial example – of the antinomy that reason will supplement – uses a peculiar thinking of what man is to put him out of it. The point is, however, that the New Hollander or the man from Tierra del Fuego *cannot* be the subject of speech or judgment in the world of the *Critique*. (*CPR* 26)

Spivak's *Critique* mimes that of Kant, trying to figure the foreclosed perspective. If, in terms of a logical matrix, the ethical would have been broached by a non-foreclosure of affect, with that foreclosure already in place, the restoration of affect can only be figured counterfactually – or by means of a literary device. That is why Spivak insists that the New Hollander or Fuegan, as she has him assume a narrative perspective, figures not a coming to speech but rather the Native Informant's foreclosure.

Like some of the works Spivak analyses in the chapter on 'Literature' (*CPR* 112–97) – J.M. Coetzee's *Foe* and Devi's 'Pterodactyl' – such counterfactual quasi-advocacy must stage as 'mute' the projected voice of the other. The performance must be of a failed ventriloquism. The one, momentary, deviation from this counterfactual rhetoric in Spivak's reading of Kant, and the most moving moment in her explication, takes place in a long footnote: '[Kant's] construction of the noumenal subject is generally dependant on the rejection [*Verwerfung*] of the Aboriginal. In German the two words are *Neuholländer* and *Feuerländer*. . . . I took these for real names and started reading about them. . . . One tiny detail may give Kant's dismissal the lie: ". . . [the] name [the Fuegans] gave themselves: *Kaweskar*, the People" ' (*CPR* 26n–29n). Roughly legible as a claim to the 'name of Man', this trace of self-naming, taken from one writer quoting another, a sign of the makings of a narrative perspective to be reconstructed by a reader, indicates a limit of this book, and the threshold of another: 'I cannot write that other book that bubbles up in the cauldron of Kant's contempt' (*CPR* 28n). But could anyone write such a book? The footnote cites linguistic competence and disciplinary and institutional obstacles, but other formulations appear to preclude 'that other book' entirely. The reasons for this take us to the heart of the practice of reading that animates *A Critique of Postcolonial Reason*, its principal contribution to a critical idiom – like Marxism, a 'globalized local tradition' (*CPR* 70) – in ethics and reading.

The intuition which guides Spivak is that, since the reader takes up, quasi-advocatively, the position of Native Informant in responding to Kant and the other philosophers, she cannot help but figure him as a reader. This tendency is, however, 'mistaken': 'there *can* be no correct scholarly model for this type of reading. It is, strictly speaking, "mistaken," for it attempts to transform into a reading-position the site of the "native informant" in anthropology, a site that can only *be* read, by definition, for the production of definitive descriptions' (*CPR* 49). In other words, in a necessary but fractured reversal of foreclosure, the reader can projectively broach affect, but cannot restore the foreclosed perspective. This is different from noting that, reading Hegel's reading of the *Srimadbhagavadgītā*, 'an implied reader "contemporary" with the *Gītā*' (though not a Hindu reader contemporary with Hegel) can be reconstituted from the text's structure of address: '[s]uch a reader or listener acts out the structure of the hortatory ancient narrative as the recipient of its exhortation. The method is structural rather than historical or psychological' (*CPR* 49–50). Whereas 'strategic complicities' (*CPR* 46) obtain between Hegel's argument and the structure of the *Gītā* in how each positions a reader, Kant's text in no way addressed, or let itself be addressed by, the Native Informant. Kant's text does nothing to open the possibility of affective or ethical relation. To imagine the Native Informant as reader, in Kant's case at least, is 'mistaken', and all that a reader can be taught is to mime his moves of foreclosure. In the case of Hegel, and the implied reader of the *Gītā*, however, 'I am calling', writes Spivak, 'for a critic or teacher who has taken the trouble to do enough homework in language and history (not necessarily the same as specialist training) to be able to produce such a "contemporary reader" in the interest of active interception and reconstellation' (*CPR* 50). This is not the same as asking, and answering empirically, such questions as: For whom was he writing? Who is the audience? Spivak's interdisciplinarity is not a sociology of reading.

If 'history' can assist with 'active interception and reconstellation', it is clear from Spivak's proviso that 'the method is structural' that any history must be answerable to an analysis of the address-structure of the text, with its own openings and foreclosures. Anything else can lead to wishful thinking. Spivak provides an alternative to the banal and potentially harmful empiricism of 'information-retrieval' (*CPR* 114, 168–71), and to unproblematized advocacy on behalf of the 'silenced'. Her method at once acts as a corrective to such contemporary tendencies in criticism, and makes it possible for us to see them as one-dimensional articulations of an original critical impulse, one for which she emerges as one of today's most profound interpreters. To read is to figure a reader; to go out of one's self, perhaps to make out a 'contemporary reader', more often than not to figure a 'lost' perspective that cannot be made out (*CPR* 65). This account of reading, scrupulously drawn from engaging the text of postcoloniality and its philosophical precursors, adds both to an older notion of reading as a process of imaginative projection, and to a more recent idiom which attends to a process of dispropriative 'invention', as instantiation of the ethical, in writing and reading.[17]

Allegory, irony and ethics

Closing her section on Kant, Spivak associates the perspective of the Native Informant, as reader, with terms from literary theory – specifically, a thematics of parabasis, irony and allegory:[18] 'To read a few pages of master discourse allowing for the parabasis operated by the native informant's impossible eye makes appear a shadowy counterscene' (*CPR* 37). In another of her splendid long footnotes, Spivak 'recommend[s] de Man's deconstructive definition of allegory as it overflows into "irony" . . . which takes the activism of "speaking otherwise" into account; and suggest[s] that the point now is to change distance into persistent interruption, where the agency of *allegorein* – located in an unlocatable alterity presupposed by a responsible and minimal identitarianism – is seen thus to be sited in the *other* of otherwise' (*CPR* 156n, cf. 430). These remarks direct us to some of the most difficult passages in Paul de Man's *Allegories of Reading: Figural Language in Rousseau, Nietzsche, Rilke, and Proust* (1979).

Concluding his reading of Jean-Jacques Rousseau's *Confessions*, at the end of the final chapter in *Allegories of Reading*, de Man borrows from Schlegel to recast allegory in terms of parabasis and irony: 'the disruption of the figural chain . . . becomes the permanent parabasis of an allegory (of figure), that is to say, irony. Irony is no longer a trope but the undoing of the deconstructive allegory of all tropological cognitions, the systematic undoing, in other words, of understanding. As such, far from closing off the tropological system, irony enforces the repetition of its aberration' (*Allegories* 300–1). Parabasis, literally a stepping-aside, refers to the intervention of the chorus in Greek drama, and to the intervention of the author in theatre contemporary with Schlegel. Glossed as '*aus der Rolle fallen*', parabasis is thus (in one sense) an interruption of the figure in performance, of an assumption of a role. It is, in other words, what fractured prosopopoeia does, stepping aside when a voice or reading-position is attributed to the Native Informant. Allegory, in one of de Man's formulations, is what disrupts continuity between cognitive and performative rhetorics. In Rousseau's *Confessions*, confession produces truth (cognitive) by disclosing the deeds of the one confessing, but undermines itself as confession when this cognitive truth functions as excuse (performative) (*Allegories* 280). De Man's remarks on allegory, irony and parabasis can be linked to his coinage and explication of 'ethicity', where the disruption of rhetorical modes appears as a disruption of two value systems.[19]

The disruption in confession turned excuse between the systems of truth and falsehood, and good and evil, is an instance of the disruption leading de Man to a rhetorical redescription of moral discourse. In rhetorical terms, the disruption generates an imperative that is referential in its bearing:

> Allegories are always ethical, the term ethical designating the structural interference of two distinct value systems. . . . The ethical category is imperative (i.e., a category rather than a value) to the extent that it is linguistic and not subjective. . . . The passage to an ethical tonality does not result from a transcendental imperative but is the referential (and therefore unreliable) version of a linguistic confusion. Ethics (or, one should say, ethicity) is a discursive mode among others. (*Allegories* 206)

Spivak takes up the referential moment as response to an imperative. By imagining the Fuegan, her reading of Kant performs the empirical, or 'ideological', transgression that de Man diagnoses in Schiller's reading of the *Critique of Judgement* (*Allegories* 16). In so doing, Spivak takes from de Man the opening provided by ethicity, which, at the end of *Allegories of Reading*, is set out in the vocabulary of allegory, irony and parabasis. The word 'allegory' comes from the Greek: *allegorein*, from *allos*, other + *agoreuein*, to speak publicly. 'Speaking otherwise' is Spivak's activist rendering. To speak – or read – otherwise in the name of that to which the philosophical example refers (which is not necessarily the empirical, since the figure is, strictly speaking, 'unverifiable'), projected as the (im)possible perspective of the Native Informant, is to perform the parabasis necessary to disrupt the inscription, in Kant onwards, of the Native Informant.[20] Interrupting informatics (cognitive, epistemic), by exposing the ideational and affective foreclosure of humanity (performative, ethical), the reader brings to light an 'ethicity' which provides the catalyst for ethics by bringing the agent before an imperative. Animating the reader with alterity, this imperative comes from elsewhere, from an other. This is how allegory is produced and staged for the NI as New Immigrant whose activity as a literary reader, Spivak hopes, will be informed by transnational literacy.

Literature and representation

In the most traditional of terms, works of narrative fiction and lyric poetry are understood to involve the reader in a process of imaginative projection and identification. Attention to this process underlies the emphasis placed in *A Critique of Postcolonial Reason* on the teaching of literature, and its ethical implications. Set down in an idiom of their own, Spivak's intuitions as a critic resonate with an impulse that has animated criticism for a long time in its formulations of the relation between beauty and goodness; between the imagination, exercised by poetry, and ethical conduct. To quote Percy Bysshe Shelley: '[a] man, to be greatly good, must imagine intensely and comprehensively; he must put himself in the place of another and of many others. . . . The great instrument of moral good is the imagination; and poetry administers to the effect by acting upon the cause' ('A Defence of Poetry' 488).

The turn toward a de Manian thematics of allegory coded in terms of irony as permanent parabasis gives Spivak and her readers a set of concepts for making sense of what, if one kept to the idiom and concerns of a Percy Shelley (whom Spivak briefly invokes [*CPR* 355n]), would amount to an interference of two systems or codes of value: beauty and goodness. In this instance, the interference would be operated by an ironic interruption of the 'main system of meaning' by the Native Informant's perspective. If putting oneself imaginatively in the place of another is indispensable to ethics, it is inevitable for a reader; if there is an opening for the ethical in reading, and for the ethical to open from reading, it is this. Spivak's point of intervention is to teach the reader to experience that place as (im)possible, as in the case of the figure she calls the Native Informant, and, in so doing, to acknowledge complicity in actuating the texts and systemic geopolitical textuality that make it so. Goodness-coding disrupts beauty-coding (cf. *CPR* 146).

The critical reader steps aside, introducing the bracketed 'im' or figuring a more or less muted prosopopoeia, and passes through, as she must, the aporia of this impossibility. Spivak's setting to work of this project in the teaching of literature is well enough known not to rehearse her readings of Brontë, Rhys, Mary Shelley and Coetzee in the chapter on Literature.[21] In order to anticipate the book's reframing of 'Can the Subaltern Speak?', which I discuss in detail in Chapter 3, I will, however, note how, although never absent, the emphasis appears to fall with added gravity on the ethical rather than on the epistemological dimension of literary figuration. This can be observed in passages added to the component texts on Mahasweta Devi's novella 'Pterodactyl', in which an advocacy-journalist in search of a story joins with Indian 'tribals' in their work of mourning the passing of the creature. There the rhetoric of thwarted prosopopoeia is framed ethically as well as affectively: 'The aboriginal is not museumized in this text. . . . This mourning [of the pterodactyl] is not anthropological but ethico-political' (*CPR* 145). To gloss this in terms of Shelley altered by way of de Man, Spivak's attention to the affective plotting of goodness-coding is, in the more recent analysis, at least as strong as truth-coding in disrupting beauty-coding. In other words, however captivating the display of the living fossil is for the viewer (and it may indeed be sublime), responsibility entails taking stock of one's position in relation to those who live.

This shift in emphasis comes through powerfully in the chapter on 'History'. The version of 'The Rani of Sirmur' included there opens, in another partaking in the work of mourning, with a transferential 'pray[er] . . . to be haunted by [the Rani's] slight ghost', and a 'miming [of] the route of an unknowing' becomes a 'mim[ing of] responsibility to the other' (*CPR* 207, 241). Pointing to an ethico-affective supplementation of the epistemic, these additions to 'The Rani of Sirmur' lead us to an altered reading of 'Can the Subaltern Speak?' In the latter, we get a disruption, in the semantics of 'representation', of the codes of truth and goodness; or, broken down more specifically, in the German of Marx's *Eighteenth Brumaire of Louis Bonaparte*, of the epistemic, the aesthetic (as *darstellen*) and the ethico-political (as *vertreten*) (*CPR* 256ff, 260, 263). Portrayal can amount to a self-delegating 'speaking for' (Arnott, 'French Feminism', 83). To separate these senses, and to expose their interested conflation, as Marx did when he wrote about tragedy being repeated as farce, is to operate an ironic parabasis. *A Critique of Postcolonial Reason* presents these involved theatrics, along with the rest of the essay's intervening matter (on Foucault and Derrida, Subaltern Studies, *sati*) as a 'digression' on the way to the 'unspeaking' of the anti-colonial activist Bhubaneswari Bhaduri, after her suicide, by other women of her social class (*CPR* 273, 309). A coda in earlier versions of the essay,[22] this unspeaking is now a portent for the (middle-class) woman of the South becoming, along with the postcolonial migrant, the agent-instrument of transnational capital (*CPR* 310, cf. 200–1), manager in a neo-colonial system which, enlisting feminist help (*CPR* 252, 255f, 259, 269, 277, 282, 287, 361, 370n), employs credit-baiting to conscript into capitalist globality the poorest woman of the South (*CPR* 6, 220n, 223n42, 237, 243n70). This is how the book tracks the itinerary of the Native Informant, and how the implied reader – also the 'newly-born . . . woman as reader as model' in 'a new politics of reading' (*CPR* 98–98n137) – is concatenated by it in a position of complicity.

When *A Critique of Postcolonial Reason* adds Bhubaneswari Bhaduri's corporate-employed great-grandniece to the chain, 'Can the Subaltern Speak?' is resituated in a history of the present written on her unspeaking. Yet the 'digression' remains indispensable to discerning the deeper current on reading underneath the Native Informant's itinerary structuring the book. Although, as Spivak observes, Bhubaneswari Bhaduri was 'a figure who intended to be retrieved' (*CPR* 246), and the survivors *interpret* her suicide, we are not dealing, in isolation, with epistemic coding, or with ethico-political coding alone, but with the permanent disruption of these and other codes in the writing Bhubaneswari left on her body. The reader does not know, or *have to* know, but rather stands aside when others, ignoring the disruptive noise of other codings, claim to know.

We can, on the one hand, as it has always invited us to (*CPR* 247), read 'Can the Subaltern Speak?' as irony in the classical mode, as *eironeia*, a Socratic questioning in feigned ignorance, provoking the law to speak[23] – as it inevitably has, ruling that of course the subaltern can speak and in the same breath contradicting its statement with vivid acts of foreclosure (see *CPR* 309; *OTM* 60–1). On the other hand, Socratic irony can itself be thought in a de Manian vocabulary of 'permanent parabasis', as a disrupting of the script of informatics through a performance of the (im)possible perspective that mimes its foreclosure of that perspective. If this disruption produces an imperative, Spivak's injunction in response appears to be: find the disruption of value systems and work at it; intervene there.

Such an ethics or politics of reading may thus be another gloss on what, from her readings of Marx, and Deleuze and Guattari, Spivak refers to in other essays as the coding, recoding and transcoding of value, a topic which continues to puzzle her ablest interpreters.[24] Involving economic, cultural and affective codes implicated in gendering (*CPR* 103ff, cf. *OTM* 281–2), and thus entering territory not explored by de Man, this is where, by analogy with the factory worker, whom Marx taught to think of himself not in terms of identity (see *OTM* 61ff), but as an agent, the implied reader-agent can acknowledge and negotiate complicity. Although not working out the details, *A Critique of Postcolonial Reason* provides clues, in the form of concrete suggestions, that help its reader to find such links in intuitions about reading and the ethical. One, from the chapter on 'Culture', is the proposal that 'a different standard of literary evaluation, necessarily provisional, can emerge if we work at the (im)possible perspective of the native informant as a reminder of alterity, rather than remain caught in some identity forever' (*CPR* 351–2). Another, from 'History', in response to United Nations efforts to 'rationalize "woman" ', concerns 'women outside of the mode of production narrative': 'We pay the price of epistemically fractured transcoding when we explain them as general exemplars of anthropological descriptions. . . . They must exceed the system to come to us, in the mode of the literary' (*CPR* 245, 245n73). Postcoloniality urges a training of the agent as reader in the literary – where the literary is that which, while it inevitably performs a referential function, is 'singular and unverifiable' (*CPR* 175) in the way it evokes and invokes an elsewhere and an other, and constantly performs disruption between aesthetico-epistemic and ethico-affective codings of representation. A paradox thus appears to emerge for a reader of *A Critique of Postcolonial Reason*: in order to read the book, the reader has to stand aside from the reading-position allocated her as declared implied reader; exceed her systemic placing when it risks gelling into yet another identity; and assume, where – unlocatably – she is, the (im)possible task of taking up what has been denied: the writing of an other life-script, which is not necessarily the same as one's own autobiography. The larger project carried forward in *A Critique of Postcolonial Reason* remains, as I read it, a work in progress, placed in the hands of its readers.

This labour has been continued by Spivak in her most recent work – which has endeavoured to link transnational literacy and an ethics of reading in a new way: literary theory in the North, literacy in the rural South. It begins to approach, perhaps, the Native Informant as a point of appropriation for 'informatics' and the relationship (visible but almost impossible to articulate in practice) between him or her and the Native Informant as postcolonial migrant or citizen.

Supplementing human rights: imagination and responsibility

From the outset, Spivak has been occupied as a critic with the trans-formation of the self. Her choice of title for her first book, *Myself Must I Remake: The Life and Poetry of W.B. Yeats*, is an early marker for this occupation. Drawing its title from Yeats's late poem, 'An Acre of Grass' (*Myself* 167), Spivak's study takes as its principal theme the unfolding of the poet's imagination, from childhood until the end of his life. Observing that Yeats 'conceived of poetry as the business of soul-making, not merely as a rhetorical exercise', Spivak concludes that '[h]is greatness lies in how serious a business poetry was for him, how totally life and poetry were conjoined in him' (*Myself* 180, 187–8).

In Spivak's more recent writings, the themes of soul-making and imaginative self-transformation that she had employed to frame the life and work of the poet have come, as I indicated in my discussion of *A Critique of Postcolonial Reason*, to be associated with other-directedness. From writing the life of the great artist, Spivak's emphasis has shifted to the project of changing the mind and desires of the reader as student of literature. In this project, the imagination becomes the link to the other and the place where the ethical relation is activated. Yet the transforma-tive connotations of remaking the self, essential to the life story of the artist, remain powerfully operative. Because it enables self-othering, the literary is, as always, the place where self-transformation may occur. Tacitly linked to the life of the artist, Spivak's ethics take on a pathos for the reader.

It is important to note that Spivak understands the project of 'soul-making' (which can be traced in name to Keats,[25] and to which she frequently alludes) to have been part of the making of the colonial subject:

> [T]he goal [in the literature classroom] is at least to shape the mind of the student so that it can resemble the mind of the so-called implied reader of the literary text, even when that is a historically distanced cultural fiction. . . . Literature buys your assent in an almost clandestine way, and therefore it is an excellent instrument for a slow transformation of the mind, for good or for ill. . . . The goal of *teaching* such a thing as literature is epistemic: transforming the way in which objects of knowledge are constructed. . . . [T]he problem of the teaching of English literature is not separated

from the development of the colonial subject. ('Burden of English' 135–40)

Spivak acknowledges this legacy as she endeavours to transform its effects.

As in a number of her analyses, the motivation for Spivak in 'Righting Wrongs', her contribution to the 2001 Oxford Amnesty Lectures series, is that the postcolonial subject, the member of the elite representing itself as Native Informant, is disconnected from the local underclasses. There is 'a real epistemic discontinuity between the Southern human rights advocates and those whom they protect' ('Righting Wrongs' 527, cf. 535). This is particularly apparent in India, where a 'class apartheid' ('Righting Wrongs' 533) separates a local elite from the rural poor. When the rural poor are *ādivāsis* or indigenous 'tribals' – sharing neither mother tongue nor religion with caste Hindus, for whom they are untouchables – the gulf separating the classes yawns even wider. When international human rights interventions are criticized for being imposed from above from the North, and there is talk about infractions of national sovereignty in the South, this class dimension is often overlooked.

Yet, according to Spivak, indigenous peoples are in touch with a responsibility-based ethics that can supplement human rights and, ultimately, even turn capitalism toward redistribution: 'the socialist project can receive its ethical push not from within itself but by supplementation from [cultural] axiomatics [that were defective for capitalism]' ('Righting Wrongs' 538).[26] She is aware that, just as the question of rights can be begged – human beings have rights according to 'natural law' – so can the question of responsibility ('Righting Wrongs' 537). This is especially so when indigenous peoples are, in dominant ethnographic generalization, classified as communitarian as opposed to individualistic. But indigenous social formations have, in Spivak's uncompromising terms, been 'stagnating', are in 'decrepitude', in a state of 'atrophy', and are 'corrupted' ('Righting Wrongs' 538, 551, 563). They have not been linked to the mainstream of historical progress. This is what makes them 'subaltern':

> I am asking readers to shift their perception from the anthropological to the historico-political and see the same knit text-ile as a torn cultural fabric in terms of its removal from the dominant loom in a historical moment. That is what it means to be a subaltern. My point so far has been that, for a long time now, these cultural scripts

have not been allowed to work except as a delegitimized form forcibly out of touch with the dominant through a history that has taken capital and empire as telos. ('Righting Wrongs' 544)[27]

Spivak explains that, for a supplementing of human rights to take place, these formations have to be made active: 'the real effort should be to access and activate the tribals' indigenous "democratic" structures to *parliamentary* democracy by patient and sustained efforts to learn to learn from below. *Activate* is the key word here. There is no tight cultural fabric ... among these disenfranchised groups after centuries of oppression and neglect' ('Righting Wrongs' 548, cf. 544).[28] This can happen by means of what she terms a 'suturing in' of 'the ethical impulse that can make social justice flourish' ('Righting Wrongs' 534, cf. 543). This repair of the 'torn cultural fabric' may, ultimately, connect people more meaningfully with the mechanisms of democracy. In the dystopia of tribal life painted by Spivak, electoral politics is corrupt: 'votes can be bought and sold here; and electoral conflict is treated by rural society in general like a competitive sport where violence is legitimate' (Righting Wrongs' 547). Spivak's goal is the formation of the rural voter through a 'training in democracy' – since rural people are the majority of the electorate in the global South, and any progressive change ultimately depends on them: 'If one wishes to make [a] restricted utopianism, which extends to great universities everywhere, available for global social justice, one must ... be interested in a kind of education for the largest sector of the future electorate in the global South – the children of the rural poor – that would go beyond literacy and numeracy and find a home in an expanded definition of a "Humanities to come" ' ('Righting Wrongs' 526).

The suturing that Spivak envisages will take place through teaching: 'Teaching is my solution, the method is pedagogic attention, to learn the weave of the torn fabric in unexpected ways, in order to suture [ethics of responsibility and democratic reflexes], not altering gender politics from above' ('Righting Wrongs' 548). Spivak concentrates on the training of teachers. The method she adopts is different from that of the anthropologist. It does not involve information-retrieval. This is, Spivak explains, why she has never spoken in detail before about her activity in rural teacher training; the academic setting demands information about the specific lineaments of the responsibility-based formation ('Righting Wrongs' 546, 548, 581n). When Spivak turns to the specifics of teacher training, she points to a legacy of rote learning in subaltern schools, distinct from the method of explanation and the emphasis placed on meaning in urban middle-class schools – the education Spivak herself received ('Righting Wrongs' 561). The emphasis on meaning is, implicitly, the stock-in-trade of the teacher of literature: not, go and memorize these words, the meaning of which is opaque to you, but, let us interpret this poem! Spivak points to an old Bengali primer by the nineteenth-century reformer Iswarchandra Vidyasagar, which advocates that the teacher of reading and writing 'jumble the structure' and foresees the pupil going on to read on his or her own ('Righting Wrongs' 552). Although the primer is still is use in the schools, its method has long been forgotten and rote learning has taken over; it took Spivak eight years to realize how Vidyasagar had intended his book to be employed by teachers ('Righting Wrongs' 554).

One of the most interesting things about 'Righting Wrongs' and other recent texts by Spivak on the subject (see, for example, 'A Moral Dilemma') is her juxtaposition of teacher training in rural India with the teaching of literature in the metropole: Columbia University in the City of New York. Although stopping short of advocating a training in the literary method of reading for human rights workers themselves ('Righting Wrongs' 532), Spivak recognizes a strong impulse among her university students to want to engage themselves in international activism. For them, such a training may be useful. It is a supplementing of human rights at two ends of the world. In 'Righting Wrongs', Spivak theorizes the consequences of a training in literary reading. She writes of a changing of minds, and of education in the Humanities as 'an *uncoercive* rearrangement of desires' ('Righting Wrongs' 526; see also 'Moral Dilemma' and ' "On the Cusp" '). This also applies to the teacher in rural India ('Righting Wrongs' 558). Added to 'transnational literacy' ('Righting Wrongs' 539), this will decentre New York City and vanguardist metropolitan human rights advocacy, and help, Spivak thinks, to create the conditions of possibility for 'learning to learn from below' ('Righting Wrongs' 537, 551) – which is a precondition for setting things to work in the rural South. Spivak envisions a 'teleo-poiesis'[29] that will, through the imagination, the singular and unverifiable, join the two ends of the globe:

> However unrealistic it may seem to you, I would not remain a teacher of the Humanities if I did not believe that at the New York end – standing metonymically for the dispensing end as such – the teacher can try to rearrange desires noncoercively . . . through an attempt to develop in the student a habit of literary reading, even

just 'reading,' suspending oneself into the text of the other – for which the first condition and effect is a suspension of the conviction that I am necessarily better, I am necessarily indispensable, I am necessarily the one to right wrongs, I am necessarily the end product for which history happened, and that New York is necessarily the capital of the world. It is not a loss of will, especially since it is supplemented in its turn by the political calculus, where . . . the possibility of being a 'helper' abounds in today's triumphalist U.S. society. A training in literary reading is a training to learn from the singular and the unverifiable. Although literature cannot speak, this species of patient reading, miming an effort to make the text respond, as it were, is a training not only in poiesis, accessing the other so well that probable action can be prefigured, but teleo-poiesis, striving for a response from the distant other, without guarantees. ('Righting Wrongs' 532)

In other recent texts, Spivak elaborates on the specific lineaments of literary reading. Her essay 'Ethics and Politics in Tagore, Coetzee, and Certain Scenes of Teaching' is an exceptional example of how a cross-disciplinary meditation on ethics can transform concepts of the literary informing literary studies. Drawing from Levinas and Derrida an account of the discontinuities between the ethical and the epistemo-logical and political, Spivak elaborates an intertextuality linking two poems by Rabindranath Tagore with J.M. Coetzee's novel *Disgrace* (1999). Spivak makes the 'general suggestion . . . that the protocol of fiction gives us a practical simulacrum of the graver discontinuities inhabiting (and operating?) the ethico-epistemic and the ethico-political' ('Ethics and Politics' 18). This produces a reading of Coetzee that concentrates on what it means, as Tagore writes in '*Apoman*', to 'have to be equal in disgrace to each and every one of those whom you have disgraced millennially' ('Ethics and Politics' 19). In the second part of her essay, Spivak moves from residual and emergent understandings of postcoloniality to 'the failure of democracy'. In so doing, she also juxtaposes, as she did in 'Righting Wrongs', two hemispheres of read-ing: comparative literature in the North, literacy in the South. She describes exchanges with students in the rural Indian schools that she views as a private supplement to state education. In both systems rote learning predominates and explanation in the service of meaning is hardly attempted by teachers. As she stages these encounters, Levinas's 'face-to-face of the ethical' materializes in the 'smile of complicity' on an intelligent student's face ('Ethics and Politics' 29). Like the literary figure, however, this is 'singular and unverifiable', yet, in its disruption of political calculus, 'an irreducible grounding condition' for ethics and politics. The two parts of Spivak's essay suggest together that a productive inter-disciplinarity may be achieved by taking the steps of literary reading – something which has political consequences when, for instance, education policy is based upon the data collected by social scientists. As Spivak acknowledges, change, if it takes place at all, will be slow and may be impermanent. Lessons may be learned in the most confused of ways, and any learned may not stick for long (see 'Ethics and Politics' 28).

In all of her work, I will argue in the chapters that follow, Spivak has pursued the articulation of a reading of the world in which transnational literacy and literary reading have gone hand in hand in adumbrating a theory of ethics and responsibility specific theoretically to the literary and tied closely, in historical terms, to the conditions of postcoloniality and globalization. Her articulation is also fundamentally interdisciplin-ary. This is readily apparent in Spivak's interventions in Marxism and feminism, which I discuss in Chapters 3 and 4. But it is nowhere more abundantly illustrated than in her activity as a translator of Jacques Derrida and Mahasweta Devi, which is the subject of the next chapter.

Notes

1   Despite the widespread influence of Spivak's work, to date it has enjoyed only a single book-length study, *Gayatri Chakravorty Spivak* (2003), a lively introduction written by Stephen Morton. Her work has, however, been discussed in some detail, though in smaller compass, by Robert Young (*White Mythologies* 157–75), Bart Moore-Gilbert (*Postcolonial Theory* 74–113) and Asha Varadharajan (*Exotic Parodies* 75–112).

2   Spivak alludes to the fiction of Salman Rushdie and others.

3   For more on the history and politics of language in Bangladesh, see Spivak's 'Translating into English' (97–9).

4   This section draws from the following: Spivak, 'Bonding in Difference' (16–17), 'Ethics and Politics in Tagore' (23), 'Foreword: On Reading the *Companion to Postcolonial Studies*' (xix–xxi), 'Lives' (211–15), 'Naming Gayatri Spivak', 'Thinking about Edward Said'.

5   For more on postcolonial theory as a field, see Young, *White Mythologies*, and Moore-Gilbert, *Postcolonial Theory*.

6   On the academic 'star system' that had emerged by the 1980s in literary studies in the United States, see Shumway. In an interview published in 1989, Spivak alludes to the way in which her career has been shaped by this system: 'I have a certain sense of how, at this point, I seem to satisfy a certain

kind of need to have a closet marginal, so I'm not troubled about the possibility of a certain kind of cultism, undeserved. . . . a great deal of my current popularity is dependent on the fact that, whether I like it or not, history is larger than my personal benevolence' ('Naming Gayatri Spivak' 87, cf. 95).

7 According to Spivak, they number 'over 80 million at last count, and [are] massively underreported in colonial and postcolonial studies. There are 300-odd divisions, most with its individual language, divided into four large language groups' (*CPR* 141). See also the documents and interview with Spivak by Anupama Rao in 'The Denotified and Nomadic Tribes of India'.

8 See also 'Diasporas Old and New'.

9 *Other Asias* is to include the essays 'Righting Wrongs', 'Responsibility', 'Moving Devi', 'Foucault and Najibullah' and 'Our Asias'.

10 On the reader of *Capital*, see also Keenan, *Fables of Responsibility* 99–133.

11 For an excellent account of 'critique', see Foucault, 'What is Critique?'

12 See Vandana Shiva, *Biopiracy* and *Stolen Harvest*.

13 'This is not to limit the readership of this essay', she says in 'Righting Wrongs', where she makes diasporics and second-generation colonial subjects her example, 'Anyone can do what I am proposing' ('Righting Wrongs' 550).

14 In *White Mythologies*, Robert Young describes Spivak's relation to conventions of positioning and oppositionality: 'Instead of staking out a single recognizable position, gradually refined and developed over the years, she has produced a series of essays that move restlessly across the spectrum of contemporary theoretical and political concerns, rejecting none of them according to the protocols of an oppositional mode, but rather questioning, reworking and reinflecting them in a particularly productive and disturbing way. . . . Spivak's work offers no position as such that can be quickly summarized. . . . To read her work is not so much to confront a system as to encounter a series of events' (157). Young contrasts Spivak's attendant 'taking "the investigator's complicity into account" ' to Edward Said's 'oppositional criticism', his 'very limited model of a detached, oppositional critical consciousness' (169, 173; the embedded quotation is in *CPR* 244).

15 We can compare this move to that of Kwame Nkrumah, who transgresses Kant's proscription of 'anthropology' to make 'the traditional African standpoint' the starting point for ethics rather than beginning with a 'philosophical idea of the nature of man' (*Consciencism* 97). The difference would be that, by preserving the moment of foreclosure in Kant – one that is indeed 'anthropological' – Spivak takes precautions to avoid the mere substitution of perspective that characterizes and sets the limits of nativism.

16 On the 'im-', Spivak directs us to 'A Literary Representation of the Subaltern', where it relates to a rhetorical question (*IOW* 263).

17 See Keenan, *Fables of Responsibility*; Attridge, *The Singularity of Literature*. The principal source texts would be Derrida, 'Psyche', and Levinas, *Otherwise Than Being* 99–129.

18 Spivak's interest in allegory dates back to some of her earliest published work; see 'Allégorie et histoire de la poésie: Hypothèse de travail', 'Thoughts on the Principle of Allegory' and *Myself Must I Remake* (184).

19 On ethicity in de Man, see Miller, *The Ethics of Reading* 41–59, Hamacher, 'Lectio' 184ff.

20 In 'Finding Feminist Readings: Dante–Yeats', thinking the feminist reader and her position is Spivak's occasion for distinguishing between deconstruction in a narrow and general sense: 'Within a shifting and abyssal frame, these [minimal] idealizations [of a work being "about something"] are the "material" to which we as readers, with our own elusive historico-politico-economico-sexual determinations, bring the machinery of our reading and, yes, judgment' (*IOW* 15).

21 Other notable readings by Spivak of individual works of fiction, by R.K. Narayan, Jamaica Kincaid, Maryse Condé and J.M. Coetzee, may be found in 'How to Read a "Culturally Different" Book', 'Thinking Cultural Questions in "Pure" Literary Terms', 'The Staging of Time in *Heremakhonon*' and 'Ethics and Politics in Tagore and Coetzee'.

22 'Can the Subaltern Speak?: Speculations on Widow-Sacrifice'; 'Can the Subaltern Speak?'

23 Like Socrates in Plato's *Apology* (414), Spivak refers to herself as a 'gadfly' (*CPR* 244). On *eironeia*, see Derrida, *Gift of Death* (76), and, on irony and the question, Derrida and Dufourmantelle, *Of Hospitality* (11–19). I offer these notes toward an account of Spivak's trajectory of irony as a hopeful corrective to Terry Eagleton's trivializing remark, in his review of *Critique*, that '[Spivak's] work's rather tiresome habit of self-theatricalising and self-alluding is the colonial's ironic self-performance, a satirical stab at scholarly impersonality, and a familiar American cult of personality' ('In the Gaudy Supermarket' 6).

24 See Young, Review 235ff.

25 In a letter to George and Georgiana Keats from April 1819, he writes: 'Call the world if you Please "The vale of Soul-making". . . . I will call the *world* a School instituted for the purpose of teaching little children to read – I will call the *human heart* the *horn Book* used in that School – and I will call the *Child able to read, the Soul* made from that *school* and its *hornbook*' (*Letters* 102).

26 The notion of ethical practices that are 'defective for capitalism' comes from Foucault's late work (see Spivak, 'From Haverstock Hill Flat' 7, 35n11).

27 Elsewhere Spivak defines subalternity as 'the space out of any serious touch with the logic of capitalism or socialism' ('Supplementing Marxism' 115).

28 See also 'Foucault and Najibullah' 224–30.

29 Spivak takes up the term from Derrida's *Politics of Friendship* (see Spivak, 'A Note on the New International' 12).

Chapter 2

Theory in Translation

Newer editions of the *Oxford English Dictionary* include an entry for the word 'deconstruction'. One of quotations appended to the entry is taken from Spivak's preface to her 1976 translation of Jacques Derrida's *Of Grammatology*:

> To locate the promising marginal text, to disclose the undecidable moment, to pry it loose with the positive lever of the signifier; to reverse the resident hierarchy, only to displace it; to dismantle in order to reconstitute what is always already inscribed. Deconstruction in a nutshell. ('Translator's Preface' lxxvii)

The paragraph from which this kernel is drawn continues: 'But take away the assurance of the text's authority, the critic's control, and the primacy of meaning, and the possession of this formula does not guarantee much.' The dictionary extracts the definition. But the translator insists on a resistance to her own textual and critical authority.

Spivak's preface to *Of Grammatology* has, for many readers, been a primer on deconstruction. If anecdote is to be credited, not all went on to read the book that it prefaces, or to read much of it. If, as one writes without thinking twice, Spivak's translation was a pivotal event in the history of Anglo-American literary theory, the erratic reception of the book that is *Of Grammatology* renders mysterious what that event was – and *is*, since its future is, in elusive ways, our present.

One way to resolve the problem of definition is to join Jane Gallop in thinking *Of Grammatology* not as Derrida's book – which runs the risk of simply reinstating the authority of the French original, *De la grammatologie* (1967) – but rather as Spivak's. In 'The Translation of Deconstruction' (1994), Gallop writes that 'in the 1990s I am more interested in Spivak than in Derrida. I began to want to read [*Of Grammatology*] as a text by Spivak rather than as a text by Derrida' (55).

Her cue to do so is a set of remarks on translation made by Spivak in her preface. 'Derrida', Spivak writes, 'use[s] the business of "mistranslations" as an effective deconstructive lever' ('Translator's Preface' lxxxvii; quoted in Gallop, 'Translation of Deconstruction' 52). To pick up on mistranslations by comparing translation with original, by holding a translation to a strict standard of fidelity to an original, can imply a highly conventional notion of translation in which the authority of the original is unquestioned. Spivak does not, however, subscribe to such a notion. As Gallop notes, when Spivak draws her preface to a close with a plea for a certain reader, she uses this lever to displace the authority of the original: 'And all said and done, that is the sort of reader I would hope for. A reader who would fasten upon my mistranslations, and with that leverage deconstruct Derrida's text beyond what Derrida as controlling subject has directed in it' ('Translator's Preface' lxxxvii; quoted in 'Translation of Deconstruction' 53).

Gallop finds in Spivak's invitation a 'translator's coup':

> Spivak's ideal reader would find her 'mistranslations' and, rather than thinking 'she should've said this because it's closer to what Derrida is saying,' the reader would stay with Spivak's word ('fasten upon it' in the sense not of catch it out but of hold to it) and think: 'that's where the text is, this is the text I want, not the one that follows Derrida's direction.' The reader would follow Spivak in her displacement of the text, rather than try to bring it back home to Derrida. The last paragraph of Spivak's Translator's Preface is a stunning articulation of active or abusive translation. At this moment she speaks not only as a translator of deconstruction but as a deconstructive translator. ('Translation of Deconstruction' 54)

To Gallop's observations, I would add the proviso that the same would, in all consistency, have to apply to Spivak's text. This would accord with the spirit of the preface, where its author draws back from definition when the *OED* will display no corresponding reserve. Without applying Gallop's argument to Spivak (as well as to Derrida), there is the risk of making the translation – just as the preface has served as a substitute for a reading of the book itself – an authority even less molested (and thus, in certain instances, more vindictively attacked) than that of the original. Gallop's enthusiasm for reading *Of Grammatology* as Spivak's book makes visible this issue but does not address it explicitly. Spivak's own pattern of self-interruption indicates how the direction of the controlling subject of her preface might be overturned.[1] As Spivak writes, 'not only is there no *Of Grammatology* before mine, but there have been as many translations of the text as readings, the text is infinitely translatable' ('Translator's Preface' lxxxvi). But perhaps a more compelling safeguard against total appropriation by the translator-author is Spivak's use of the old word 'mistranslation'. On the one hand, as Gallop suggests, for Spivak it is the mistranslation rather than the faithful translation that brings the authority of the original to crisis. It is, one assumes, the glaring mistranslation that leads one to consider the original, and, ultimately, to reconsider its status. In all rigour, though, would a correct translation not also lead one in this direction if one were reading translation and original side by side? If it would, Spivak's message could be somewhat more complex. One might then see all translations, in relation to what they translate, as 'mistranslations'. Spivak suggests this when she asks: 'If there are no unique words, if, as soon as a privileged concept-word emerges, it must be given over to the chain of substitutions and to the "common language," why should that act of substitution that is translation be suspect?' ('Translator's Preface' lxxxvi). When the translation is neither any less nor any more open to the displacements of intertextuality than the original, one must, in all consistency, maintain a vigilance vis-à-vis *both* texts. This is an outcome that seems consistent, ultimately, with Gallop's reading.

A second movement in Gallop's discussion of Spivak is to regard *Of Grammatology* as a work in postcolonial theory. As a text by Spivak rather than by Derrida, would it, appearing two years before Edward Said's *Orientalism*, be postcolonial theory's founding work? When Gallop fastens on Spivak's criticism of Derrida's near 'reverse ethnocentrism' – 'the *East* is never seriously studied or deconstructed in the Derridean text' ('Translator's Preface' lxxxii, quoted in 'Translation of Deconstruction' 55) – which she groups with Spivak's critique of Julia Kristeva's *About Chinese Women* in 'French Feminism in an International Frame' (1981), she declares herself to have been influenced by postcolonial theory. It has changed the way she reads the French texts from the 1960s and 1970s ('Translation of Deconstruction' 55–8). Without elaborating, Gallop suggests that when one embraces ' "active translation" ' and 'reread[s] the original from the point of view of the context into which it has been translated. . . . [Spivak's 1987 book] *In Other Worlds* might also be thought of as Spivak's translation of Derrida' ('Translation of Deconstruction' 58). Postcolonial theory may be viewed as an experiment in reading the world – or, as the subtitle of *A Critique of Postcolonial Reason* has it, in writing a history of the vanishing present. If so, the 'context' to which Gallop refers exceeds turf battles between university professors of modern languages.[2]

If postcolonial theory as it has taken shape in the writings of Spivak is a translation of deconstruction in the sense that Gallop thinks, then the implications of this 'translation' can be generalized beyond the reading and rereading of the seminal texts of French theory. As Sandhya Shetty and Elizabeth Jane Bellamy point out in 'Postcolonialism's Archive Fever' (2000), when Spivak discusses *sati* in 'Can the Subaltern Speak?', it is *Of Grammatology* that leads her back to the Sanskrit archive and its errors of transcription and translation that lead to the locution: the *sati* wanted to die (see *CPR* 287). That is the archive upon which the colonial legal codification builds when it silences the female subaltern through an imperialist benevolence that Spivak, miming Freud's ' "A Child is Being Beaten" ', phrases as: 'White men are saving brown women from brown men' (*CPR* 284). If the hieroglyphist prejudice of the West leads to an uncritical celebration of Eastern systems of writing, and Derrida's exposure of this prejudice, in turn, to an essentialization of the West, 'Can the Subaltern Speak?' tries both to undo the prejudice and continue its deconstruction. Although Shetty and Bellamy do not refer to Gallop's essay, their argument can be elaborated in dialogue with Gallop's thoughts about translation. Each translation leads to a questioning of the original. If British legal codification in India is one such translation, and it is found to be a more or less obvious and interested mistranslation (*CPR* 303), it will not do to stop there. We need to interrogate the original – which is not an 'orientalist' construct, be it so translated in colonial laws against *sati* or in French theory.

This is the rethinking at stake in the translation of deconstruction announced in Spivak's preface. Gallop ends her essay by mentioning briefly Spivak's translations of Bengali writer Mahasweta Devi. For Gallop, the main issue is that the difference in status between Derrida and Devi within the metropolitan academy means that, in each case, the original will have a correspondingly different authority. This is where the politics of translation is a politics of mediation. I would argue, though, that the experience of translating Devi has changed, or at least led to develop, in crucial ways, Spivak's thinking of translation. Fiction emphasizes, perhaps more than does philosophy – which pursues truth – the operation of the unverifiable figure. It also shows how the text shades into the social, how it engages a heteroglossia of social struggle. Translating Devi's fiction has led Spivak to the unverifiable as that which calls for response. Practice has transformed theory. In 'The Task of the Translator' (1923), Walter Benjamin famously affirmed it as desirable that a translation allow the language of the original to transform that of the translation. Translation ought to be transformative. This has also been Spivak's guiding orientation as a translator. Yet there is a difference: that transformation is reciprocal; the original, on being revisited, will never be the same; it will no longer have a monopoly on transformation.

After surveying Spivak's writing on Derrida as a way of entering into the idea of translation as a special case of reading, I will turn to her reflections on translating Devi and the ways in which they inform her conception of a new comparative literature.

Spivak's Derrida

Spivak has written illuminating commentaries on nearly all of Derrida's major works. Her preface to *Of Grammatology* was followed by essays in *Diacritics* in the 1970s and 1980s on *Glas*, *La Carte Postale* and *Limited Inc*. More recently, she has published discussions of *Of Spirit: Heidegger and the Question*, *Specters of Marx*, *Circumfession* and *Politics of Friendship*. These essays could, and apparently will, comprise a book of their own.[3] To say that Spivak's work has developed in close dialogue with Derrida's would be an understatement. In the three chapters that follow, I track the influence of deconstruction on Spivak's contributions to Marxism, feminist theory and to an analysis of the current global conjuncture that combines elements of both modes of analysis. In the present chapter, I explore this itinerary by taking up the theme of translation.

The appendix to *A Critique of Postcolonial Reason* is an indispensable index to Spivak's understanding of the trajectory of deconstruction and its implications for literary, cultural and political theory. Entitled 'The Setting to Work of Deconstruction', it supplies a compact account of the evolution of Derrida's thinking. An English rendering of '*mise en oeuvre*', 'setting to work' itself suggests translation of a certain kind. Spivak identifies a decisive turn towards ethics:

> At the conference entitled 'The Ends of Man' held in 1982 [*sic*] at Cerisy-la-Salle,[4] Derrida described a movement in his own work. . . . It was a turn from 'guarding the question' – insisting on the priority of the unanswerable question, the question of *différance* – to a 'call to the wholly other' – that which must be differed-deferred so that we can posit ourselves, as it were. As we have seen in our discussion of radical alterity in 'Différance,' a

similar double program was figured in his work from the start. The movement now announced by Derrida – understood as an other-directed swerve away from mere philosophical correctness, alerts us to a greater emphasis on ethics and its relationship to the political. (*CPR* 425–6)

From early on, Spivak's reading of Derrida – which has amounted to an active translation – concentrated on the differed-deferred other required for the self to posit itself. After drawing out the implications of Derrida's critique of ethnocentrism near the end of her preface to *Of Grammatology*, Spivak began devoting her analyses to the figure of 'woman' and the scope and limits of Derrida's deconstruction of phallocentrism.[5] Like her noticing of an implicit ethnocentrism in Derrida himself, her explication of his subsequent works poses a challenge to the authority of the original in the name of 'woman' who, although subversive of the law for the male philosopher, is, ultimately, doubly displaced. By pursuing the implications of Derrida's texts from a reading-position unanticipated by them – which may be what makes translation not only necessary but possible – Spivak anticipates the turn that is later made explicit by Derrida himself when he entertains the call to the wholly other.[6]

When Spivak first proposed a translation of *De la grammatologie*, she insisted on writing a 'monograph-size introduction' ('Gayatri Spivak on the Politics of the Subaltern' 86). Tracking affinities between Derrida and Nietzsche, Heidegger, Freud and Husserl, and the relation of Derrida to structuralism and to Lacanian psychoanalysis, and emphasizing Derridean motifs of erasure, writing and the trace, Spivak's preface is an attempt to explicate Derrida genealogically and thematically. The subsequent review essays continue this task, but gradually develop an understanding and critique of Derrida's work that is Spivak's very own.

Founded in 1970, the journal *Diacritics* has made the genre of the extended review essay its speciality. Opening its pages to Spivak over nearly three decades, during which it has published four of her most important essays on Derrida, the first three in the space of seven years, *Diacritics* has fostered her extended commentary on and dialogue with his work. The first step was Spivak's meticulous reading of *Glas* (1974), Derrida's striking two-columned book that, in mourning the father and putting autobiography in his empty place, juxtaposes the family in Hegel's speculative philosophy with the fiction of Jean Genet, sexual and criminal breaker of the law. '*Glas*-Piece: A *compte rendu*' (1977) indicates two paths of reading that are pursued in nearly all of Spivak's subsequent writing on Derrida. The first, as the appendix to *A Critique of Postcolonial Reason* would lead us to suspect, concerns the setting to work of deconstruction. In a coda to '*Glas*-Piece', Spivak writes, looking toward the future: 'After *Glas*, he seems more systematically occupied with the exploration of the textuality of the *hors-texte* – the thing, the act' (43). This will relate, as I show in the next chapter, to Spivak's Derridean rereading of Marx.[7]

The second path follows Derrida's critique of phallogocentrism in *Glas*, and is a critical feminist commentary on it and subsequent works by Derrida. In Derrida's occupation with the Freudian discourse on the fetish, Spivak explains, a 'rewriting of a certain Oedipianized psycho-analysis frames *Glas*. . . . If the fetish can mean both the castration and the non-castration of the mother, the knell (*glas*) of the law (*logos*) of the phallus as transcendental signified is sounded' (28, 31).[8] In 'Love Me, Love My Ombre, Elle' (1984), her discussion of *La Carte Postale: de Socrate à Freud et au-delà* (1980), Spivak 'suggest[s] that it is possible to say that "woman" on the scene of Derrida's writing, from being a figure of "special interest," occupies the place of a general critique of the history of Western thought' (22). Here the play of 'woman' in philosophy – as fetish, hymen, veil and the other figures that disrupt logocentric closure – begins to be criticized: 'does such a "generalization" of woman negate "woman in the narrow sense?" . . . [Derrida] cannot show his readers womankind made heterogeneous by many worlds and many classes' (24n9, 35). In 'Displacement and the Discourse of Woman' (1983), a commentary on Derrida's *Éperons/Spurs* (1978), and a return to *Glas* with references to *Dissemination* and 'The Law of Genre', Spivak argues that in Derrida's critique of phallocentrism the figure of woman is 'doubly displaced'. When he writes, explicating Nietzsche, that ' "[t]here is no essence of woman because woman averts and averts herself from herself. . . . For if woman *is* truth, *she* knows there is no truth, that truth has no place and that no one has the truth" . . . Derrida interprets . . . [this] double displacement into the sign of an abyss. But perhaps the point is that the deconstructive discourse of man (like the phallocentric one) can declare its own displacement (as the phallocentric its placing) by taking the woman as object or figure. . . . man can prob-lematize but not fully disown his status as subject' ('Displacement' 173). Thus there is a displacement, but woman remains an object or figure *for the male philosopher*. The figure of woman deconstructs phallocentrism – but does so *from the subject-position* of man. The alternative, for the feminist critic, is:

to rewrite the *social* text so that the historical and sexual differentials are operated together . . . to notice that the argument based on the 'power' of the faked orgasm, of being-fetish, and hymen, is, all deconstructive cautions taken, 'determined' by that very political and social history that is inseparably co-extensive with phallocentric discourse. . . . this rewriting of the social text of motherhood cannot be an establishment of new meanings. It can only be to work away at concept-metaphors that deliberately establish and cast wide a different system of 'meanings'. ('Displacement' 185)

This is what Spivak had made of the figure of clitoridectomy in 'French Feminism in an International Frame' – generalizing in terms of the 'effacement of the clitoris' the reproductive inscription of woman's body ('Displacement' 190).[9]

It is important to note that, despite her reservations about Derrida, Spivak does not privilege feminism *against* deconstruction. One instance is her concluding response to the papers presented at a 1986 conference, 'The Difference Within: Feminism and Critical Theory'. Sensing that speakers at the conference had been presenting ' "post-structuralism" ' or ' "post-modernism" ' as an 'enemy', Spivak reminds them that their subject-position as feminist academics depends on a forgetting of the history of the institution. Her response is to lecture the participants on the Derridean trace: 'What is the trace? The trace is like this: whenever you construct any kind of discourse, describing feminism . . . if you look at it you will see that at the beginning of the discourse, in order to be able to speak . . . there was something like a two-step. The two step was the necessity to say that a divided [*sic*] is whole. . . . We must cover over the trace of the history of the Western institution in order to speak as feminists' ('Response' 211). In her preface to *Of Grammatology*, the trace is one of Spivak's principal topics ('Translator's Preface' xv–xviii). In a similar vein, in 'Feminism and Deconstruction, Again: Negotiations' (1989), Spivak actually draws back from her critique of Derrida in 'Displacement and the Discourse of Woman': 'today, negotiating, I want to give the assent for the moment to Derrida's argument [in *Éperons/Spurs*]. Affirmative deconstruction says "yes" to a text twice, sees complicity when it could rather easily be oppositional' (*OTM* 128–9).

Apart from her texts on Derrida and Marx, which I discuss in Chapter 3, and her brilliant exposition of *Of Spirit* in 'Responsibility' (1994), Spivak's commentaries on later texts of Derrida – such as 'Circumfession' and *Politics of Friendship* – are, although rigorous and insightful,[10] not as striking as some of her earlier explications and position-taking. This is, to my mind, because Spivak has so thoroughly elaborated a critical idiom of her own in an intimate reading of Derrida's writings that the explicit commentary that positions her in relation to them is in fact less productive than the paths of thinking and writing that have been facilitated for her through this – to use Spivak's term – 'critical intimacy'. That said, however, there remains a recognition of her own writing as a setting to work of deconstruction.[11]

One of the most moving and apposite things to have been said in the memorial writings published after Jacques Derrida's death on 9 October 2004 is Spivak's reminder that he, like Marx, was a teacher of global reach. In making that take place, translation played no small part:

> There can be no doubt that Derrida knew more than most of us about teaching – from the intimacy of a small seminar in French to the long distance and remote spectrality of the Internet; from English to the many languages of the world. . . . A single teacher's students, flung out into the world and time, is a real-world example of the precarious continuity of Marxism in the lowest reaches of global activism today. There is often a slow but tenacious change of mind, quickly dismissed by the metropolitan establishment. ('Remembering Derrida' 15)[12]

Translating Mahasweta Devi

In her practice as a translator of Mahasweta Devi's fiction, and in her commentary on that practice, Spivak has pursued relentlessly her analysis of the social text as it situates women. In 'The Politics of Translation' (1992) Spivak writes that '[t]he task of the feminist translator is to consider language as a clue to the workings of gendered agency' (*OTM* 179). This is where the politics of translation resides. Without such attention, readers of Third World literature receive 'a sort of with-it translatese, so that the literature by a woman in Palestine begins to resemble, in the feel of its prose, something by a man in Taiwan' (*OTM* 182). The feminist translator must thus consider language, or '(agency in) language' as threefold: logic, rhetoric and silence (*OTM* 183, 181). Silence is the limit before which even the rhetorical and figural must acknowledge their incapacity to make meaning. That limit, residing in any language, in any source or target language, is important to Spivak as a limit to translation in general (*OTM* 181). But, in the specific consideration of gendered agency that Spivak advocates, it is to the play of logic and rhetoric that she devotes the greater attention. For this is where the actual practice of translation takes place.

The title of Mahasweta Devi's story 'Stanadāyini' (1980) is one example. Spivak translates it as 'Breast-Giver' (*OTM* 182). The title of an alternative published translation, 'The Wet-nurse', Spivak argues, 'neutralizes the author's irony in constructing an uncanny word; enough like "wet-nurse" to make that sense, and enough unlike to shock. . . . The theme of treating the breast as organ of labor-power-as-commodity and the breast as metonymic part-object standing in for other-as-object – the way in which the story plays with Marx and Freud on the occasion of the woman's body – is lost even before you enter the story' (*OTM* 182–3).[13] It is Devi's irony that renders visible the workings of gendered agency – here the labour-power of the breast figured as *gift*, a sign, perhaps, of 'internalized gendering perceived as ethical choice' (Spivak, 'Translator's Preface' to *Imaginary Maps* xxviii; see also *IOW* 264–7).[14] Devi's title is an instance of how this construction of agency may be challenged, of the 'disruptiveness of figuration in social practice' (*OTM* 187). Spivak stresses the fact that Devi is 'unlike her scene', and thus provides a way of questioning the reverse ethnocentrism of uncritically celebrating Third World women's writing, where the possibility exists that 'what seems resistant in the space of English may be reactionary in the space of the original language' (*OTM* 189, 188). In order to translate, then, the translator must be mindful of literary history: '[t]he history of the language, the history of the author's moment, the history of the language-in-and-as-translation, must figure in the weaving as well' (*OTM* 186).[15] Again, the authority of the original is challenged when the translator follows its rhetoricity: what is its relation to its *social* text?

Spivak's essay 'A Literary Representation of the Subaltern' (1987) elaborates this question. 'Breast-Giver' tells the story of Jashoda, who, for three decades, suckles generations of children from the wealthy Haldar household, exchanging her breast milk for food for her and her husband, who was crippled after being run over by a car driven by the youngest Haldar son. After discovering a lump in her breast, which remains untreated, Jashoda dies of cancer. Jashoda is imbued with ideas of herself as carrying out the prophecy of, even embodying, the Mother Goddess. The narrator of Devi's story is explicit about the baneful consequences for her of accepting this script:

> Jashoda is fully an Indian woman, whose unreasonable, unreasoning, and unintelligent devotion to her husband and love for her children,

whose unnatural renunciation and forgiveness have been kept alive in the popular consciousness by all Indian women. . . . One must become Jashoda[16] if one suckles the world. One has to die friend-less, with no one left to put a bit of water in the mouth. . . . Jashoda was God manifest. . . . Jashoda's death was also the death of God. When a mortal masquerades as God here below, she is foresaken by all and she must always die alone. (*IOW* 225–40)

The most dramatic move in Spivak's essay, first presented at a 1986 Subaltern Studies conference at which Mahasweta Devi was present, is that it reads against the grain of the author's own interpretation of her story as:

a parable of India after decolonization. Like the protagonist Jashoda, India is a mother-by-hire. All classes of people, the post-war rich, the ideologues, the indigenous bureaucracy, the diasporics, the people who are sworn to protect the new state, abuse and exploit her. If nothing is done to sustain her, nothing given back to her, and if scientific help comes too late, she will die of a consuming cancer. (*IOW* 244)

For the story to be read as a parable, the subaltern must be the meta-phoric vehicle for the nation. This means, Spivak argues, that 'what must be excluded from the story is precisely the attempt to represent the subaltern as such' (*IOW* 244). Devi, in other words, is not doing justice to her own story, in which the representation of Jashoda makes her any-thing but representative of India. Spivak's intervention is entirely in the spirit of Subaltern Studies, whose exponents had worked to displace elite colonial and nationalist historiography with a study of the move-ments and insurgencies of underclass groups.[17] As Ranajit Guha writes, such history writing 'fails to acknowledge, far less interpret, the contri-bution made by the people *on their own*, that is, *independently of the elite*, to the making and development of nationalism' ('On Some Aspects' 39; also see *IOW* 245). Although Subaltern Studies has undertaken a project of writing history from below, when Devi speaks about her story, evi-dently not all of the historians are prepared to question the author's interpretation (*IOW* 268).

Spivak's reading of 'Breast-Giver' positions itself between Devi as the story's author and the metropolitan reader who 'homogenizes the Third World and sees it only in the context of nationalism and ethnicity' (*IOW* 246), a benevolent liberal feminist reader with whom the author, interpreting her story as a parable of the nation, is effectively complicit

(*IOW* 246, 254). The position of that reader shades into that of the metropolitan migrant intellectual (*IOW* 256–7) – the NI of *A Critique of Postcolonial Reason* (see also Devi, ' "Telling History" ' xvii). Approaching 'Breast-Giver' through a Marxist feminism and, in turn, through Lacanian psychoanalysis, Spivak sheds light on different elements of the story (*IOW* 247–63). Spivak concludes with considerations of gendering – where she returns to Devi's narrator's comment that 'Jashoda is fully an Indian woman, whose unreasonable, unreasoning, and unintelligent devotion to her husband and love for her children, whose unnatural renunciation and forgiveness have been kept alive in the popular consciousness by all Indian women from Sati-Savitri-Sita through Nirupa Roy and Chand Osmani' (*IOW* 225). By adding her to a chain of figures from Sanskrit epic and Hindu mythology to stars of Bollywood film, 'Mahasweta presents Jashoda as constituted by patriarchal ideology' (*IOW* 265). Spivak is at pains to show, however, that this does not make Jashoda the parabolic representative of an exploited India. In order to do this, Spivak presents a careful and complex explication of 'Breast-Giver' as metafiction – of 'the story in literary history rather than the stream of reality' (*IOW* 266). Despite this staging of Jashoda, Spivak argues:

> The end of the story undoes [the] careful distancing of the author from the gender-ideological interpellation of the protagonist. . . . It is the three propositions at the very end that call into question the strategically well-advertised ironic stance of the author-function.
>
> The language and terminology of these conclusive propositions remind us of those high Hindu scriptures where a merely narrative religion shifts, through the register of theology, into a species of speculative philosophy: 'Jashoda was God manifest, others do and did whatever she thought. Jashoda's death was also the death of God. When a mortal plays God here below, she is forsaken by all and she must always die alone.' (*IOW* 266)[18]

It is at this crucial juncture that Spivak introduces the concept of *translation*. It forms the bridge between the labour of representation of the writer of fiction and that of the Subalternist writer of history, who argues that 'the subaltern as historical subject persistently translates the discourse of religion into the discourse of militancy' (*IOW* 266). An analysis of the figure of Gandhi by Shahid Amin is one example of Subaltern Studies scholarship that follows this particular process of translation. 'Breast-Giver' can enter into conversation with the historian (see *IOW* 244) because it records a failure of such translation:

If . . . the story (*enoncé*) tells us of the failure of a translation or discursive displacement from religion to militancy, the text as statement (*énonciation*) participates in such a translation (now indistinguishable from its 'failure') from the discourse of religion into that of political critique.

'Stanadayini' as statement performs this by compromising the author's 'truth' as distinct from the protagonist's 'ideology.' Reading the solemn assenting judgement of the end, we can no longer remain sure if the 'truth' that has so far 'framed' the ideology has any resources without it or outside it. (*IOW* 266)

The tasks of translator and critic are united in Spivak's endeavour to question the author's interpretation of her work in the cause of resisting the homogenization of Third World literature by women. This homogenization can take place through an acting out of an ambivalence well articulated by Gallop: 'Although I feel uncomfortable or unsettled . . . about Spivak's displacement of Mahasweta Devi, I am rooting for and enjoying Spivak's displacement of Jacques Derrida. I seem to be playing out my ambivalence about translation's relation to the original by projecting it onto this binary opposition: it's good to do it to this guy, it's bad to do it to this woman' ('Translation of Deconstruction' 59). Simply to play (or act) out such an ambivalence would impose a double standard, the effect of which would be to trivialize the work of Third World women writers. For Spivak, writing as Devi's translator, there can be no such double standard. If national allegory is the going literary-critical counterpart to 'with-it translatese', Spivak's careful labours as a critic complement her translations by complicating Devi's relation to her background.[19]

Some of Spivak's most striking insights come from a return to the representation of the subaltern in Devi's story. This representation is bound up with the 'workings of gendered agency'; in 'Can the Subaltern Speak?' *representation*, as an articulation of *portrayal* and *substitution*, is a necessary precondition for agency as institutionally validated action. This, as I outline below, also involves 'translation'. When, in 'The Politics of Translation', Spivak alludes to the disruptiveness of the *figure* in social practice, and says that she favours Mahasweta because she is unlike her context, we have the tip of an iceberg. 'The Politics of Translation', an essay frequently anthologized, must be read over against 'A Literary Representation of the Subaltern' for us to see how Devi's critique of the workings of gendered agency is, in terms of the rhetorical conduct of her text, implicated in those very workings. In de

Manian terms, to which Spivak is very close in both these essays without being always explicit, Devi's text produces an allegory of unreadability – acting out a perpetual disruption of performative and constative, or of the two senses of 'representation' that are the preoccupation of Spivak's intervention in Marxist politics in 'Can the Subaltern Speak?'[20] Representation is a species of translation. The failure of that translation, as staged in a literary work such as 'Breast-Giver', is continuous with that active in the social text – here, with the dynamics of subaltern insurgency. We witness what Mikhail Bakhtin termed a heteroglossia. Reading 'Breast-Giver' as a parable elides the complex 'representation' of the subaltern in insurgency. Doubling representation as translation in the social text, Spivak's translation of Devi's story and her commentary on it restore some of these lines of connection.

Spivak's practice as a translator has changed. Has a change in practice meant a change in theory? In order to address this question, I turn to her most recent translation of Mahasweta Devi's work, *Chotti Munda and His Arrow* (2003). Originally published in Bengali in 1980, Devi's novel tells the story of the eponymous 'tribal' leader and the vicissitudes of life for the Mundas from early in the twentieth century through Indian independence and the Emergency declared by Indira Gandhi in the 1970s, when the Naxalite armed insurgency drew support among tribals, who pass down stories of the anti-colonial uprising led by Birsa Munda late in the nineteenth century. Perennially subject to bonded labour, the Mundas forge an existence by continually negotiating and renegotiating agreements with landowners and local officials and police. Chotti Munda, a master archer but loath to use his arrow to take human life, is the figure about whom this fragile, and not infrequently violent, *modus vivendi* turns.

The language of *Chotti Munda and His Arrow* reveals a new and audacious departure in Spivak's practice as a translator. In the foreword to her 1981 translation of Devi's story 'Draupadi', Spivak had written about how Devi's representation of Bengali as spoken by tribals had posed a challenge to the English of her translation:

> I have had the usual 'translator's problems' only with the peculiar Bengali spoken by the tribals. In general we educated Bengalis have the same racist attitude toward it as the late Peter Sellers had toward our English. It would have been embarrassing to have used some version of the language of D.H. Lawrence's 'common people' or Faulkner's blacks. Again, the specificity is micrological. I have used 'straight English,' whatever that may be. (*IOW* 186)

If, in 'Draupadi', the speech of tribals is translated into 'straight English', what is striking about *Chotti Munda and His Arrow* is the invention of a new tongue. Noticeable in this argot is a vocabulary that includes American slang and colloquialism, and transliterated Bengali including lexicalized loan words from English.[21] Phonetically, it is characterized by a constant elision of final consonants and vowels. Here is an exchange, from early in the novel, between Dhani Munda and a police officer:

> Why're ye jerkin' t' Mundas aroun' at market and takin' cuts?
> Who said?
> I say. Daroga must be told. If ye cross t' Mundas – takin' cuts again! Understan'? Then Daroga too will hafta answer. Yes, I'll not tease t' Munda people. But e'en t' Gormen don' want new torture and t' Munda roughed up. (*Chotti Munda* 6)

This transformed English, because spoken by no living human being, is, in all rigour, a 'dialect' only in the loosest sense. Would this not also apply, however, if the dialogue were in Bengali, the original language? Spivak appears to recognize this, in a general way, in 'The Politics of Translation' when she describes her practice as a translator:

> At first I translate at speed. If I stop to think about what is happening to the English, if I assume an audience, if I take the intending subject as more than a springboard, I cannot jump in, I cannot surrender. . . . Surrendering to the text in this way means, most of the time, being literal. When I have produced a version this way, I revise. I revise not in terms of a possible audience, but by the protocols of the thing in front of me, in a sort of English. And I keep hoping that the student in the classroom will not be able to think that the text is just a purveyor of social realism if it is translated with an eye toward the dynamic staging of language mimed in the revision by the rules of the in-between discourse produced by a literalist surrender. (*OTM* 189–90)

That a translation emerges first as an 'in-between discourse' that imposes its own protocols and has a life of its own would surely also apply to invented subaltern languages in Lawrence or Faulkner. The fact that their characters are based on people who actually speak English is not an essential difference. Seen from this perspective, is there really cause for the embarrassment of which Spivak writes in the foreword to 'Draupadi?' There might indeed be if it *is* racism that shapes the discourse. If racism is something outside of the control of the intending subject, however, the surrender in translation which Spivak describes may indeed allow it to speak. When she translated 'Draupadi', Spivak insured her translation against this risk by using 'straight English'. This convention is retained, on the whole, in the stories translated in *Imaginary Maps*. But her inventiveness in *Chotti Munda and His Arrow* is so radical that it becomes a point of concern for her and a matter to be raised with the author. 'One of the most striking characteristics of the novel', Spivak writes, 'is the sustained aura of subaltern speech, without the loss of dignity of the speakers. It is as if normativity has been withdrawn from the speech of the rural gentry. For the longest time I was afraid to attempt to translate this characteristic' (*Chotti Munda* vii). The fruit of her attempt is the idiosyncratic argot which I quoted briefly above. Spivak is delighted by Devi's response on reading it: ' "Gayatri, what I am really enjoying in your translation is how you've shown that dialect can be dignified." ' Shown! It was she who had "shown" this in the text and created a test of faith for me' (*Chotti Munda* vii). If in this countersignature there is not a reinstating of the authority of the author that is challenged in 'A Literary Representation of the Subaltern' there is a sense in which the translator has learned from the writer that the miming that produces 'a sort of English' is not unlike that which produced the Bengali of the original. Writer and translator play the same game, and take the same risk: that the autonomy or unverifiability of the in-between discourse freed from the original and its subsequent elaborations will not be credited, and that it will be read (that is: praised/condemned) as if it were a 'socially symbolic act' in the most restricted of senses.[22] Devi as a writer becomes an ally in resisting a narrowly activist politics of reading. That what is at stake for them is the 'dignity' of the subaltern and his or her speech – a topic coming up a number of times in the conversation between Devi and Spivak (*Chotti Munda* ix–xxiii) – does not get us to the bottom of the matter. Suggesting something about the relation or non-relation of the elite intellectual to the subaltern tribal (there is, Devi says in *Imaginary Maps*, 'no point of contact' [xxii]) it might, I would surmise, be a place-marker for the ethical in the sense of what, in 'Responsibility' (19), Spivak stages as the constant annulling of responsibility in its setting to work. The aporia of the ethical in the indeterminacy of communication is a persistent theme in Spivak's commentary on Devi's novella 'Pterodactyl, Pirtha, and Puran Sahay', which she translated for inclusion in *Imaginary Maps* (1995). In the story, Puran, an advocacy journalist, visits a starving tribal village where, miraculously, a live pterodactyl has appeared. The creature reveals to him the dynamics of advocacy as a general predicament; as Spivak writes: 'The pterodactyl is not only the ungraspable other but also the ghost of the ancestors that haunts our present and our future. We must learn "love" (a simple name for ethical responsibility-in-singularity), as Puran does in "Pterodactyl", in view of the impossibility of communication. We cannot even and after all be sure that the pterodactyl *has a* message for us. Yet we must think that it wants to speak' (*Imaginary Maps* 200–212n8).[23]

Translation is a work in progress, and theory does not always catch up with its practice – even when what is being translated is 'theory', as in the case of *Of Grammatology*. Yet, there is perhaps a tacit theory of 'dignity' in what Spivak has written on translation in recent years. Although in Spivak one finds a near constant oscillation – from her foreword to *Of Grammatology* to her texts on Devi – between the idea of text as substitutive economy without 'original' and of text as social through-and-through and possessing a singularlity and idiomaticity before which the translator is responsible, there are ways of articulating these two reaches of oscillation.

In 'Translation as Culture' (2000), one of the most recent chapters of what Emily Apter thinks of as a 'translation book that has never been framed as such' ('Afterlife' 204), Spivak takes up the work of psychoanalyst Melanie Klein in order to generalize and reorient the concept of translation. This makes it possible for her to articulate the work of the translator at her text, with the everyday displacements that make for agency in the social text – whether, to assemble our themes, it be 'female agency', 'subaltern militancy', or the production of 'dignity'. All are comprehensible as instances of the genesis of ethical responsibility as described by Klein in her revision of Freud and the Oedipus complex begun in the 1930s in *The Psycho-Analysis of Children* (1932) and continued in a large number of subsequent essays. Klein's key concept, introduced in order to explain the development of conscience (or superego) in early infancy, is *reparation*. According to Klein, the infant makes reparation, in symbolic fashion, for damage that it has done in phantasy, in retaliation for being deprived of nourishment, to the maternal breast. The infant's relation to this part-object becomes the basis for its relation to the mother, then the father, and ultimately to all others, including itself as other (see, for instance, Klein, 'Love, Guilt and Reparation'). Introducing the word 'translation', one not operative in Klein's text, Spivak provocatively explicates Klein in highly synthetic fashion:

Melanie Klein ... suggested that the work of translation is an incessant shuttle that is a 'life.' The human infant grabs on to some one thing and then things. This grabbing (*begreifen*) of an outside indistinguishable from an inside constitutes an inside, going back and forth and coding everything into a sign-system by the thing(s) grasped. One can call this crude coding a 'translation.' In this never-ending weaving, violence translates into conscience and vice versa. ... Thus 'nature' passes and repasses into 'culture,' in a work or shuttling site of violence ...: the violent production of the precarious subject of reparation and responsibility. ... In this understanding of *translation* in Melanie Klein, therefore, the word *translation* itself loses its literal sense, it becomes a catachresis. ... In the sense that I am deriving from Klein, *translation* does indeed lose its mooring in a literal meaning. Translation in this general sense is not under the control of the subject who is translating. Indeed the human subject is something that will have happened as this shut-tling translation, from inside to outside, from violence to conscience: the production of the ethical subject. This originary translation thus wrenches the sense of the English word *translation* outside of its making. ('Translation as Culture' 13–14)

If the 'subject of reparation and responsibility' is produced through the process of translation that Spivak draws from Klein, then it is a simple matter to observe that, in a general sense, translation is a power-ful (even if catachrestic) concept for making sense of the production of, say, the subject of subaltern militancy – which shuttles in and out of the figural language and 'regulative psychobiography' offered by religion – and that of female agency – which, to some extent, does the same in Devi's 'Breast-Giver'. It is highly important, as Spivak emphasizes, that this process is not under the control of the intending subject. Translation is originary in the sense of there being no original – if 'original' is understood as something existing prior to translation. It is a trace in a series of traces. As a human being, I exist only by virtue of this incessant transfer. Yet, on the other hand, there is, in the psychic appar-atus, a 'force' that, as Derrida observes in 'Freud and the Scene of Writing', 'institutes translatability, makes possible what we call "lan-guage," transforms an absolute idiom into a limit which is always already transgressed' (*Writing and Difference* 213).

In a fascinating aside, Spivak writes that 'translation in the narrow sense ... is also a peculiar act of reparation – toward the language of the inside, a language in which we are "responsible," the guilt of seeing it as one language among many. . . . I translate from my mother tongue' ('Translation as Culture' 14). Yes – but when she translates Devi, Spivak also translates from her mother tongue as spoken by people for whom it is not a mother tongue. What does it mean to be responsible to that tongue? This, I believe, is what is at stake for Devi and Spivak when they exchange words on 'dignity'. If 'dignity' is the worth or worthiness of someone, we have value-coding, the outcome of a Kleinian shuttling or oscillation between good and bad breast, and all that it entails for the production of the subject of responsibility. With talk of 'dignity' we have a making-good (*Wiedergutmachung* was Klein's word when she still published in German). Translation is reparation – not only for the mother but for the one who will never have been the mother, who never could have been the mother, and for whom 'dignity' (and such terms) are the symbolic forms of repair made in a language that he or she will never have spoken and never have understood. 'Dignity' *in* translation. The complexity of their exchange is abyssal. The word 'racism' stands impotent before it and the non-relation that translation both acknowledges and defies.

Deconstruction, translation and the new comparative literature

Spivak's translations of Devi's fiction are posed as an alternative to the translatese pervasive in world literature – that literature that circulates, away from its context of production, and is read in translation.[24] Blind to local literary history and an author's difference within it, the international translation industry homogenizes, producing the literature of the Third World as a simplified literature (see *IOW* 267, *OTM* 182). Spivak has tied her aims as a translator to the idea of a 'New Comparative Literature'. In its inception, this idea is linked, as it is in her commentaries on Mahasweta Devi, to a transformative setting-to-work of deconstruction. Because Comparative Literature as an academic discipline 'may have kept deconstruction moored to its European provenance, even in its radicalism. . . . [and] has also kept deconstruction's interest in sexual difference at an uneasy distance from the male-dominated centre of high comparatism . . . the imperative to re-imagine Comparative Literature is also an imperative to re-imagine deconstruction' ('Deconstruction and Cultural Studies' 22). When the East is imagined as an *area* of study and the global South is objectified, deconstruction can encourage a response in ethical singularity by attending to idiomaticity of language and codes of cultural production: 'Engagement with the idiom of the global other(s) in the Southern hemisphere, uninstitutionalized in the Euro–US university structure except via the objectifying discontinuous tourist-gaze of anthropology and oral history, is the displaced lesson of Deconstruction and Cultural Studies' ('Deconstruction and Cultural Studies' 30). Translation is thus at the centre of this nexus of deconstruction, cultural studies and comparative literature.

Spivak has in mind more than the work of individual translators. In terms of institutional arrangements, advocating a translation from the South that honours idiom has meant for Spivak an alliance with Area Studies. The latter, an artifact in the United States of a Cold War geo-politics that divided the world into strategic 'areas' of study, has, Spivak believes, always maintained a rigorous standard for the learning of the language or languages necessary for a scholar to conduct research in a particular 'area' (*Death of a Discipline* 7). Combined with Comparative Literature's methods of close reading,[25] this practical commitment to the learning of languages outside of its traditional geographic purview has the potential to revolutionize Comparative Literature (*Death of a Discipline* 9). The New Comparative Literature will fulfil the promise of the discipline 'to include the open-ended possibility of studying all literatures, with linguistic rigor and historical savvy' (*Death of a Discipline* 5). Spivak's ideas are currently being put into practice at Columbia University, where Spivak was the force behind the establishment in 1998 of a Centre for Comparative Literature and Society, an initiative promoting exchanges between departments of 'national' languages and literatures (English, French, German and so forth), and other humanities departments, with the social sciences, and schools of law and architecture. The goal, in all of this, remains a certain project of translation – the one generalized, as in 'Translation of Culture', through Melanie Klein: 'In order to reclaim the role of teaching literature as training of the imagination – the great inbuilt instrument of othering – we may, if we work as hard as old-fashioned Comp. Lit. is known to be capable of doing, come close to the irreducible work of translation, not from language to language but from body to ethical semiosis, that incessant shuttle that is a "life" ' (*Death of Discipline* 13).

Notes

1 On the subject of interruption, see Spivak's remarks in *The Post-Colonial Critic* (44). Also see Bal, 'Three-Way Misreading' (19–20), for a hint that this pattern comes from teaching.

2 Some would argue that those battles are, however, the condition of possibility for postcolonial theory. See, for instance, Dirlik, 'The Postcolonial Aura'.

3 *Of Derrida*, forthcoming.

4 The correct date is 1980.

5 Though not actually undertaking it, the preface anticipates this subsequent work: 'In what it seems satisfying to me to construe as a ~~feminist~~ gesture, Derrida offers us a hymeneal fable' ('Translator's Preface' lxvi).

6 Commenting on his essay 'Violence and Metaphysics: An Essay on the Thought of Emmanuel Levinas' (1964), Derrida remarks in response to a paper by Jean-Luc Nancy: 'At bottom it is the word of *question* that I would have changed there. I would have displaced the accent of the question towards something that would have been call [*appel*]. Rather than a question that one must guard, a call (or an order, desire or demand) that one must have heard' (Lacoue-Labarthe and Nancy, *Les fins de l'homme* 184). In a footnote in *Outside in the Teaching Machine*, Spivak relates that '[i]n the actual discussion, which was considerably longer than what is transcribed in the book, the contrast between preserving the question and calling to the wholly-other was sharper' (*OTM* 303n5).

7 It also relates to 'Revolutions That As Yet Have No Model' (1980), Spivak's second piece on Derrida in *Diacritics*.

8 For more on the fetish in *Glas*, see 'Displacement and the Discourse of Woman' 177–9, 183–4.

9 I discuss 'French Feminism in an International Frame' in more detail in Chapter 4.

10 See 'Three Women's Texts and *Circumfession*', 'Deconstruction and Cultural Studies', 'A Note on the New International' and 'Poststructuralism Meets Schmitt: Schmitt Meets Poststructuralism: A Response'.

11 'My relationship to "deconstruction," whatever that may be, has become more intimate, more everyday, more of a giving – away, and in – habit of mind, a kind of tic that comes in to warn in the thick of what is called activism, formulas that guide in the midst of those who have little or nothing' ('Ghostwriting' 65).

12 Spivak makes the same point in 'Deconstruction and Cultural Studies' (34) and in 'A Note on the New International' (13).

13 In the 'Introduction' to *Breast Stories* (1997), which assembles her translations of 'Breast-Giver', 'Draupadi' and 'Behind the Bodice', Spivak turns, as she has increasingly in more recent work, to Melanie Klein in order to explicate Devi's psychoanalytic play: 'In 1986, writing on "Breast-giver," I had invoked Lacan. I did not then know of a generally unacknowledged debt [of

Lacan] to Melanie Klein' (xiv). Spivak can be critical of Devi's Marxism: 'The Marxian fable of a transition from the domestic to the "domestic" mode of social reproduction has no more than a strained plausibility here. In order to construct it, one must entertain a grounding assumption, that the originary state of "necessary labor" is where the lactating mother produces a use value. For whose use? If you consider her in a subject-position, it is a situation of exchange, with the child, for immediate and future psycho-social affect' (*IOW* 250).

14 'In "Breast-Giver," [the breast] is a survival object transformed into a commodity, making visible the indeterminacy between filial piety and gender violence, between house and temple, between domination and exploitation' ('Introduction' to *Breast Stories* vii).

15 This also applies in 'The Politics of Translation' to a song to Kāli written in the eighteenth century by Ram Proshad Sen, of which Spivak examines two different renderings – both of which appear in her translation accompanying twentieth-century artist Nirode Mazumdar's *Song for Kali* (2000). For more on Mazumdar and Ram Proshad, see 'Moving Devi' (144–7). As Spivak writes in 'Translating into English' (2005), the translator must also be mindful of an author's presuppositions (93–4).

16 As Spivak explains, 'The mythic mother of Krishna, and in that sense the suckler of the world' (*IOW* 240n).

17 Spivak's sympathetic critique of the group is contained in 'Subaltern Studies: Deconstructing Historiography' (*IOW* 197–221).

18 The rendering of the final proposition differs slightly in the published version of the translation included in *In Other Worlds*: 'When a mortal masquerades as God here below, she is forsaken by all and she must always die alone' (*IOW* 240).

19 As Spivak writes more recently, 'The only way to get rid of *translatese* is to feel the authority as well as the fragility of the "original," by way of resonance with its irreducible idiomaticity' ('Questioned on Translation' 21).

20 See Chapter 1 for more on Spivak's use of de Man.

21 These loan words were not italicized, as they were in *Imaginary Maps*, in the published version of *Chotti Munda and His Arrow* (see *Chotti Munda* vii–viii). In *Imaginary Maps*, the difficulty of reading a text with these italicized words is seen by Spivak as 'a reminder of the intimacy of the colonial encounter' (xxxi).

22 The term 'socially symbolic act' alludes to the subtitle of Fredric Jameson's book, *The Political Unconscious: Narrative as a Socially Symbolic Act* (1981).

23 There is further commentary on 'Pterodactyl' in *A Critique of Postcolonial Reason* (140–6). Spivak includes an important essay on another of the stories in *Imaginary Maps*, 'Douloti the Bountiful' in *Outside in the Teaching Machine* (77–95). She discusses the third story, 'The Hunt', in 'Who Claims Alterity?'

24 I take this definition from Damrosch, *What is World Literature?* (4).

25 Of course, not all comparatists share a commitment to close reading. See
    Moretti, 'Conjectures', and Spivak's response to him (*Death of a Discipline*
    107–9n1).

Chapter 3

Marx after Derrida

In 1993, Jacques Derrida published *Specters of Marx: The State of the Debt, the Work of Mourning, and the New International.* Theorists on the Left had waited a long time for Derrida to engage with the work of Karl Marx. Thinkers influenced by deconstruction had, to be sure, produced innovative departures in Marxist theory. But what most people had awaited was not Marxism after deconstruction but,[1] in some sense, the authorized Marx after Derrida. What they received was a fascinating but oblique account of the figure of the spectre in Marx's oeuvre, concentrating on his early works – *The German Ideology, The Manifesto of the Communist Party* and *The Eighteenth Brumaire of Louis Bonaparte* – rather than on the three volumes of *Capital: A Critique of Political Economy.* Derrida's reading of these texts, in conjunction with analyses of Heidegger and *Hamlet,* is explicitly presented as a meditation on the legacy of Marx after the end of Soviet Communism. Messianic themes drawn from Walter Benjamin are developed by Derrida into the idea of a New International and 'democracy to come'. Responses to *Specters of Marx* were as mixed as expectations for the book had been high.[2]

Gayatri Chakravorty Spivak's 'Ghostwriting' (1995), published in *Diacritics,* is highly critical of Derrida's book on several counts. Her principal criticism is Derrida's failure, according to her, to distinguish between commercial and industrial capital. This is the pivotal distinction made by Marx in volume one of *Capital,* published in 1867. Spivak has, in one way or another, made this criticism of Derrida since 1980, and continues to do so ('Remembering Derrida' 20). But, in 'Ghostwriting', it is couched in a sarcasm exceptional in Spivak's writings on Derrida: 'I have always had trouble with Derrida on Marx. A friend said maybe that's because I feel proprietorial about Marx. Who knows? Maybe. At any rate, I have laid out my trouble in print . . . My main problem has been Derrida's seeming refusal to honor the difference between indus- trial and commercial capital' ('Ghostwriting' 65). The tone of Spivak's essay was enough to provoke from Derrida an indignant response.[3] There may have been, on Spivak's part, a certain frustration that, more than a decade after her intervention at the 1980 colloquium at Cerisy, 'Les fins de l'homme: à partir du travail de Jacques Derrida', where she first pointed it out, Derrida is still making the same mistake. And, what is more, it is not simply a mistake by the standards of Spivak's reading of Marx, but, ultimately, a failure by Derrida himself to carry through his own method of reading when it comes to the Marxian text. Spivak explicitly shows that her reading of the distinction between commercial and industrial capital is guided by a Derridean thematics. The pupil honours the teacher, but the teacher remains deaf to the pupil. Not only will Derrida not be the pupil, he will not even acknowledge the lesson.

Spivak's insistence on the difference between commercial and industrial capital – which, as she explains, Marx did not understand right away – is interconnected with her understanding of the concepts of *use value* and *exchange value* in *Capital*, volume one. It is also related, for Spivak, to the mammoth question of the transition from capitalism to socialism – a topic broached by Marx at the end of *Capital*, volume three, edited and published by Frederick Engels in 1894, more than ten years after Marx's death. This network of differences – industrial/commercial capital; use value/exchange value; capitalism/socialism – continues to animate Spivak's pathbreaking writings on Marx. It lies at the centre of her search for an *ethical* supplement to *Capital*. Over many years, Spivak returns to the topic of use value several times in slightly different ways. Typically, the received understanding of use value is that it eludes the circuit of exchange: things can be available for use and not be commodities. According to Spivak, this received notion of use value, though widely entertained by non-Marxists and Marxists alike, does not do justice to what Marx actually wrote in *Capital* – where use value is at the basis of his concept of *labour power*. What is consistent about Spivak's writings on Marx is their use of Derrida to explicate the Marxian text.

As Spivak declares in 'Speculation on Reading Marx: After Reading Derrida' (1983/1987), when she writes on Marx, she 'turn[s] to a cherished set of texts after having read a new set' ('Speculation' 30). Her published work on Marx first appeared in the years immediately following the appearance of her translation of *Of Grammatology* in 1976. Spivak dates the genesis of 'Speculation on Reading Marx' to 1978 ('Speculation' 42), making it, in some sense, the earliest of her pieces on Marx, rather than the Cerisy intervention, which was published in French in 1981 and translated into English and revised for inclusion in *Outside in the Teaching Machine* in 1993.

In 'Speculation on Reading Marx', Spivak is very clear about how her approach to Marx has been guided by Derrida. 'To force a reading of Marx through Derrida', she writes, 'opens up the textuality of the economic' ('Speculation' 43). Major themes of her 'Translator's Preface' to *Of Grammatology* are in evidence. Taking as her point of departure a footnote of Derrida's to his essay 'White Mythology: Metaphor in the Text of Philosophy' (1971), Spivak explains how in the *Grundrisse*, Marx's notebooks of 1857–58, money behaves like a supplement: 'Money is the mark of the principle of alienation already immanent in property. . . . It is precisely this necessary and immanent alienation, the ever-recuperable chain of the negation implicit in immanent contradiction, that Derrida approaches with the open-ended graphic of supplementarity. . . . And once money is seen as an unrecognised supplement in Marx, it shows all the marks of writing' ('Speculation' 33). Spivak proceeds to show how Derrida 'can be used to deconstruct the opposition between use- and exchange-value in the same way' ('Speculation' 36). This leads her from money and the circuit of exchange, the subject matter of the *Grundrisse*, to *Capital* and the sphere of production. There one finds 'the necessary and essential super-adequation of labour-power to itself: it is in the nature of labour-power to create more value than it consumes' ('Speculation' 38). In *Capital*, Spivak argues, exchange value is a text and a representation. It has, in other words, a differential character. This means that use value, which Marx defines as what is left over when exchange value is subtracted from the thing, is a theoretical fiction ('Speculation' 40). Spivak here refers to 'the definitive passage in the canon': 'In the exchange-relation of commodities their exchange-value appears to us as totally independent of their use-value. But if we abstract their use-value from the product of labour, we obtain their value, as it has just been defined. The common element that represents itself [*sich darstellt*] in the exchange-relation or exchange-value of the commodity, is thus value' (*Capital* 1: 128). This is a passage to which she will return repeatedly over the years.

Adding to the motifs of writing and supplementarity the Derridean occupation with the 'proper', Spivak approaches the crux of her essay. '[I]s it possible', she asks, 'to locate an itinerary of the improper in Marx?' ('Speculation' 49). This question has, in part, already been answered – in her analysis of the *Grundrisse*. In the context of *Capital*, however, the question is more pointed because it concerns labour-power: 'free human labour can be appropriated by capital because it too can be im-proper to itself. . . . the distinguishing *property* of labour-power is to be improper, in excess of self-adequation' ('Speculation' 53). This observation leads Spivak to a remarkable set of observations on the relationship of labour power to use value:

> The itinerary of the im-proper in Marx also runs through that end-and-origin term, use-value, against which is posed the contingent circuit of exchange value. 'The usefulness of a thing makes it a use-value . . . The very body of the commodity is therefore a use-value. Thus its characteristic does not depend on whether the appropriation of its useful properties [*Gebrauchseigenschaften*] cost men little or much time. . . . Use-value realises [*verwirklicht*] itself only in use or consumption' [*Capital* 1: 126]. But this body of the commodity . . . signifies an exchange-situation between man and nature. It is a 'good' exchange, perpetrated by the concrete individual, before the 'bad' exchange organized by abstraction has set in. . . . Here again Derrida's argument from supplementarity helps us. If a hierarchical opposition is set up between two concepts (identity/relationship, use-value/exchange-value), the less favoured or logically posterior concept can be shown to be implicit in the other, supply a lack in the other that was always already there. . . . The opposition between use-value and exchange-value can be deconstructed, and *both* can be shown to share the mark of impropriety. The category of use-value is emptied of its archeoteleological pathos when it is used to describe the relationship between capital and labour-power. The capitalisation of living labour is the realisation of the use-value of labour *seen as a commodity by capital*. ('Speculation' 54–5)

In 'Speculation on Reading Marx', Spivak is not yet using this understanding of labour power, as she does in subsequent essays on Marx, to frame a difference between industrial and commercial capital. But she is employing it to underline the peculiar nature of labour power as a commodity. Its double nature is of major importance in apprehending the specificity of the political and ethical implications of *Capital*. Because, as Marx writes, 'the extraction of surplus-value . . . "is a piece of good luck for the buyer [of labour-power: the capitalist], but by no means an injustice towards the seller [of labour-power: the worker]" [*Capital* 1: 301] . . . [a] purely *philosophical* justification for revolutionary practice cannot be found' ('Speculation' 50). Elsewhere Spivak notes in parentheses that Marx did not hold that the capacity of free human labour to be appropriated by capital 'come[s] about with capitalism; [rather] capitalism rationalises it for the purposes of the self-determination of capital' ('Speculation' 53). According to Spivak, Marx's text does not fully draw these conclusions. It remains caught up in the opposition of alienated labour and the work that one does for oneself. It takes a Derridean reading, Spivak argues, to unlock the essential impropriety of labour that will entail an ethics and politics that must, ultimately, let go of philosophical justice in the name of 'social or revolutionary justice' ('Speculation' 53).

Another way in which Spivak takes up Derrida in 'Speculation on Reading Marx' deserves mention. Discussing Marx's critique in the *German Ideology* of Stirner's 'equating [of] so-called synonyms', Spivak emphasizes that 'the first moves of deconstruction were made by noticing what happened when the synonymity/identity of the "same" word allowed contradictory or asymmetric messages to be disguised as a unified argument' ('Speculation' 35). Spivak could be alluding to 'writing' in the text of Western metaphysics, as Derrida analyses it in *Of Grammatology*. Repeated elsewhere (*IOW* 155), this point becomes the pivot about which 'Can the Subaltern Speak?' moves when, in a reading of Marx's *Eighteenth Brumaire*, it distinguishes two senses of the word 'representation' that are regularly conflated by theorists. This I examine in some detail below after considering other key texts of Spivak on Marx.

At the colloquium on Derrida held at Cerisy in 1980, Spivak turns her insights into use value in Marx into a critique of Derrida. In 'Limits and Openings of Marx in Derrida' (1993), an expanded and revised version of the essay published in the proceedings *Les fins de l'homme* in 1981, Spivak frames her critique as she does in 'Ghostwriting': 'Derrida seems not to know Marx's main argument. He confuses industrial with commercial capital, even usury; and surplus-value with interest produced by speculation' (*OTM* 97). Spivak notices 'some important uses of the metaphors of money and political economy in Derrida's texts' (*OTM* 103/'Il faut' 508). As in 'Speculation on Reading Marx', she receives her cue to attend to these metaphors from Derrida himself: 'To attend to privileged metaphors in a philosophical text is of course a lesson learned from Derrida' (*OTM* 103/'Il faut' 508). A key instance for Spivak is a passage from Derrida's 'Restitutions of the Truth in Pointing', a dialogic text from *The Truth in Painting* (1978) on Heidegger's essay 'The Origin of the Work of Art'. Derrida concentrates on Heidegger's thoughts on Van Gogh's paintings of shoes. Spivak comments on the following passage: 'Denuding of the shoes that have become bare things again, without utility [*utilité*], stripped of their use-value? . . . The naked thing (*blosse Ding*) is a sort of product (*Zeug*) but a product undressed (*entkleidetes*) of its being-as-product' (*Truth in Painting* 300, quoted in *OTM* 105/'Il faut' 509). 'The absence of the term "use-value" ', Spivak argues, 'in Heidegger's commentary on Van Gogh and the fact that the two voices apparently dialoguing in "Restitutions" seem here to be one another's iteration make it probable that this use of "use-value" is endorsed by Derrida' (*OTM* 105/'Il faut' 509). Spivak points out that there is 'no such thing as subtracting use-value from a thing' in Marx's account of production in *Capital* (*OTM* 105). Derrida, according to Spivak, 'ignor[es] the specificity of the discourse of the critique of political economy' (*OTM* 106/'Il faut' 510). She thus explains in detail the relation in *Capital* between use value and surplus value: '[C]apital "constantly drives beyond its own limits" by consuming the use-value of human labor-power, fluid abstract average labor. Capital cuts this flow by consuming its use-value. In full-dress: labor-power as commodity is sublated into (exchange[able]) value by being negated as use-value' (*OTM* 106/'Il faut' 510).[4] As in 'Speculation on Reading Marx', Spivak suggests the political implications of her analysis of use value, this time updating it (the final two sentences of the following passage were added in 1993) with a telegraphic synopsis of the transition from capitalism to socialism and the Marxian aporia of work and commodity:

> Surplus-value (more-worth) in Marx marks the necessary superadequation of the human to itself. . . . there is no *philosophical* injustice in the *Verhältnis* of capital. Capital is only the supplement of the *natural* and *rational* teleology of the body, of its irreducible capacity for superadequation, which it uses as use-value. Capital*ism* manages the contradictions inherent in capital in its own interest. In order for his dream of the social to be calculated into Social*ism* managing the contradictions of Capital in the interest of the socially human, Marx must therefore not only not emphasize the opposition between work and commodity (an emphasis for all 'human'ist theories of reification), but use their common double nature as commodity for an active calculus. (*OTM* 107/'Il faut' 510).

There is thus a great deal at stake when, in texts published in the 1970s, Derrida appears to have ignored the specificity of political economy and, '[i]ndeed, nearly fifteen years later, after many subtle changes in his thinking, Derrida seems not to have advanced his grasp of surplus-value' (*OTM* 111). In those intervening years, however, Spivak was not idle. In 'Scattered Speculations on the Question of Value' (1985), she develops further the insights of her two earlier essays.[5]

This time Spivak approaches the question of value from the key Marxist concept of 'primitive accumulation' or 'original accumulation'. In *Capital*, Marx employed this concept to find a way out of the never-ending circle of money being transformed into capital, capital into surplus value, and surplus value back into capital: 'But the accumulation of capital presupposes surplus-value; surplus-value presupposes capitalist production; capitalist production presupposes the availability of considerable masses of capital and labor-power in the hands of the commodity producers' (*Capital* 1: 873, quoted in *IOW* 160). As Spivak observes, Marx 'resolves [the discontinuity] by invoking a process rather than an origin' (*IOW* 160). 'So-called primitive accumulation', Marx writes, 'is nothing else than the historical process of divorcing the producer from the means of production' (*Capital* 1: 874–5, quoted in *IOW* 161). In a decisive paragraph, Spivak distinguishes her interpretation of *Capital*, not only from dominant Marxist notions of primitive accumulation, but also from Marx's own idea that this is simply a historical process. For Spivak, that historical process is underwritten by a historical *possibility*:

> When . . . capital is fully developed – the structural moment when the process of extraction, appropriation, and realization of surplus-value begins to operate with no extra-economic coercions – capital logic emerges to give birth to capital as such. This moment does not arise either with the *coercive* extraction of surplus-value in pre-capitalist modes of production, or with the accumulation of interest capital or merchant's capital. . . . The moment, as Marx emphasizes, entails the *historical* possibility of the definitive predication of the subject as labor-power. Indeed, it is possible to suggest that the 'freeing' of labor-power may be a description of the social possibility of this predication. Here the subject is predicated as structurally superadequate to itself, definitively productive of surplus-labor over necessary labor. And because it is this necessary possibility of the subject's definitive superadequation that is the origin of capital as such, Marx makes the extraordinary suggestion that Capital consumes the *use*-value of labor-power. (*IOW* 161)

Spivak proceeds to outline, in more detail than in either 'Speculation on Reading Marx' or 'Limits and Openings of Marx in Derrida', what the political implications of her analysis are. Again, she contrasts philosophical to social justice:

If the critique of political economy were simply a question of restoring a society of use-value, this would be an aporetic moment. 'Scientific socialism' contrasts itself to a 'utopian socialism' committed to such a restoration by presupposing labor outside of capital logic or wage-labor. . . . Indeed, it may perhaps be said that, in revolutionary practice, the 'interest' in social justice 'unreasonably' introduces the force of illogic into the good use-value fit – *philosophical* justice – between Capital and Free Labor. If pursued to its logical consequence, revolutionary practice must be persistent because it can carry no theoretico-teleological justification. It is perhaps not altogether fanciful to call this situation of openendedness an insertion into textuality. The more prudent notion of associated labor in maximized social productivity working according to 'those foundations of the forms that are common to all social modes of production' is an alternative that restricts the force of such an insertion [*Capital* 3: 1016]. (*IOW* 161)

Subsequent writings by Spivak on Marx explore in various ways this 'insertion into textuality' in order to discover an ethics that will, in the name of socialism, supplement the philosophical justice of *Capital*. In 'Ghostwriting', she again points to 'the secret of industrial capitalism: the creation of surplus value through labor-power as commodity. . . . Labor-power as commodity is the ghostliness of the body' (72–3). Working in and out of *Specters of Marx* and other works by Derrida, constantly adding and underlining her corrections to them, Spivak writes in a dense passage: ' "The origin of exchange-value is [*not*] the birth of capital" [*Specters* 147]. It is no more than the *possibility* of capital; surplus-value is the birth of capital – "the gift supplement" understood not in terms of "surplus-values as the necessity . . . to return with interest" but as the definitive predication of the human [Derrida, *Given Time* 24]. Socialism could be described as the winning back of the gift supplement into responsibility' ('Ghostwriting' 77). Summing up her writings of the early 1990s on this question (see 'Supplementing Marxism'; *OTM* 107ff), where socialism is increasingly viewed as the *différance* of capitalism, Spivak writes that:

[i]t is only [when the worker grasps work as socialized average abstract labor] that the fetish character of labor-power as commodity can be grasped and can become the pivot that wrenches capitalism into socialism. . . . Marx did indeed ignore something: that the differantial play between capital-ism and social-ism was a case of a

more originary agon: between self and other; a differantiation perhaps necessary for the business of living, a differantiation that may
be described as the *fort-da* of the gift of time in the temporizing of
lives. ('Ghostwriting' 68)

It is these reflections that lead Spivak to a new series of meditations
on how Marxism can be supplemented in responsibility. For ideas and
practices of responsibility that may be able to perform this, Spivak
turns, on the one hand, to Melanie Klein ('Ghostwriting' 68, 70) and
Levinas ('From Haverstock Hill' 11); and, on the other, to the 'ghost
dance' ('Ghostwriting' 70) and those social formations 'defective for
capitalism', to which she alludes in 'Righting Wrongs' and explores, as
I discuss in the last section of this chapter, with specific reference to
Marx in 'From Haverstock Hill Flat to U.S. Classroom, What's Left of
Theory?' (2000).

In the latter essay, which closely examines in detail Frederick Engels's
editorial presence in *Capital* in order to explicate questions of labour
power and use value in more detail ('From Haverstock' 1–7), the impres-
sion that Spivak is criticizing or correcting Derrida is less pronounced.
So too is the scrupulous acknowledgment of a debt to deconstruction, or
any bid for recognition from the master. The insights stand alone, and
one has no doubt about the originality and brilliance as contributions to
Marxist theory of this text and the ones that preceded it, beginning in
the early 1980s with 'Speculation on Reading Marx', 'Limits and Openings of Marx in Derrida' and 'Scattered Speculations on the Question
of Value'.

What is not as frequently noted is how, dating from the same time,
'Can the Subaltern Speak?' is a subtle meditation on Marxist political
theory. First drafted in 1982–83, and then presented at the Marxism and
the Interpretation of Culture conference at Champaign-Urbana in the
summer of 1983 organized by the Marxist Literary Group,[6] the essay
for which Spivak is best known emerged at a time when her return to
Marx after Derrida (see 'Speculation' 30) was at its height, and emerged
for a Marxist audience. In 'Can the Subaltern Speak?', to be sure, there
are references to the international division of labour and to the exploitation of workers in the periphery. But the main Marxist focus is *The
Eighteenth Brumaire of Louis Bonaparte* (1852) and its treatment of 'representation'. What is hardly ever noticed is how this reading is linked to
Spivak's reading of Marx through Derrida – namely, to the exposure of
the same word being used to conflate different concepts in order to
make an argument succeed when it otherwise could not.[7] What is

usually missed, in effect, is how Marxism, for Spivak, becomes a setting-to-work of deconstruction.

'Can the Subaltern Speak?'

In 'Can the Subaltern Speak?' Spivak explores the implications, for a left politics, of the conflation of two senses of representation. I produce a restricted summary of what, when the essay is revised for inclusion in *A Critique of Postcolonial Reason*, is presented as part of a long 'digression' (*CPR* 247) to the suicide of Bhubaneswari Bhaduri and its interpretation by her female relatives. Spivak begins with a conversation from 1972 between Michel Foucault and Gilles Deleuze published as 'Intellectuals and Power' (*Language, Counter-Memory, Practice* 205–17). When Deleuze declares that ' "[t]here is no more representation; there's nothing but action" – "action of theory and action of practice which relate to each other as relays and form networks" ', he is making the important point that 'the production of theory is also a practice'. 'But', Spivak continues, 'Deleuze's articulation of the argument is problematic. Two senses of representation are being run together: representation as "speaking for," as in politics, and representation as "re-presentation," as in art or philosophy' (*CSS* 275/*CPR* 256). When this takes place, '[t]he critique of ideological subject-constitution within state formations and systems of political economy can . . . be effaced, as can the active theoretical practice of the "transformation of consciousness" ' (*CSS* 275/*CPR* 257). This twofold effacement underlies left intellectuals' image of 'self-knowing, politically canny subalterns . . .; representing them, the intellectuals represent themselves as transparent' (*CSS* 275/*CPR* 257). This effect, in turn, prompts the question: *can* the subaltern speak? Spivak's strategy – '[i]f such a critique [ideological subject-constitution] and such a project ["transformation of consciousness"] are not to be given up' – is to work from out of Marx's *Eighteenth Brumaire*, in which she analyses 'the play of *vertreten* ("represent" in the first sense) and *darstellen* ("re-present" in the second sense) . . . where Marx touches on "class" as a descriptive and transformative concept' (*CSS* 275–6/*CPR* 257). To take up one turn in Spivak's analysis – which anticipates the reframing of 'Can the Subaltern Speak?' as the second part of the chapter on 'History' in *A Critique of Postcolonial Reason* – let us observe how Spivak frames the relation between descriptive and transformative conceptuality in terms of an 'older debate: between representation or rhetoric as tropology and as persuasion. *Darstellen* belongs to the first constellation, *vertreten* – with stronger suggestions of substitution – to the second' (*CSS* 276/*CPR* 259). This can also be understood in terms of the relation between constative and performative (cf. *CPR* 283). 'Again', Spivak continues, '[*darstellen* and *vertreten*] are related, but running them together, especially in order to say that beyond both is where oppressed subjects speak, act, and know *for themselves*, leads to an essentialist, utopian politics' (*CSS* 276/*CPR* 259).[8] This, as an updated example tells us, 'can, when transferred to single-issue gender rather than class, give unquestioning support to the financialization of the globe, which ruthlessly constructs a general will in the credit-baited rural woman even as it "format"s her through UN Plans of Action so that she can be "developed"' (*CPR* 259). In the earlier version, although a terminological shift to tropology and persuasion takes place (*CSS* 277/*CPR* 260), the implications of the analysis for radical intellectual practice as set out there remain, to my mind, within a problematics of *Darstellung*; the critic's task is to *expose* what lies behind verbal representations: 'The complicity of *vertreten* and *darstellen*, their identity-in-difference as the place of practice – since this complicity is precisely what Marxists must *expose*, as Marx does in *The Eighteenth Brumaire* – can only be appreciated if they are not conflated by sleight of word' (*CSS* 277/*CPR* 260; my emphasis).

Things are, I would propose, altered when 'Can the Subaltern Speak?' is reframed and revised in *A Critique of Postcolonial Reason*. Intensifying allusions via the vocabulary of tropology and persuasion to Paul de Man's later writings, what is *understood* (the essay as a performance has always seemed to exceed this understanding) in the earlier version as *exposure*, and a questioning of interested representation, is rewritten as 'permanent parabasis'. A majestic footnote in the chapter on 'Literature' hints at this transformative translation: distance (between signifier and signified) is turned into persistent disruption, as Spivak 'recommend[s] de Man's deconstructive definition of allegory as it overflows into "irony" . . . which takes the activism of "speaking otherwise" into account; and suggest[s] that the point now is to change distance into persistent interruption, where the agency of *allegorein* – located in an unlocatable alterity presupposed by a responsible and minimal identitarianism – is seen thus to be sited in the *other* of otherwise' (*CPR* 156n). In Chapter 1 I went into the critical intimacy of Spivak with *Allegories of Reading* and other texts by de Man that yields this formulation. Here it must suffice to note that, apart from his phrasing of allegory (or speaking-otherwise) in terms of irony as parabasis (in dramatic terms, *aus der Rolle fallen*) (*Allegories* 300–1), de Man sets out allegory of reading as, among other textual predicaments, the disruption of performative and constative (or cognitive, as he tends to call it). Here, as in other instances, Spivak's use of de Man is *transformative*: *ethicity* as rhetorical predicament (*Allegories* 206) turns into rhetoricity as an engagement of the ethical. Though not equivalent, the distinction and interference between rhetoric as persuasion and as tropology appears to belong to the same series. So too does the complicity of portraiture and proxy in representation as *darstellen* (constative) and *vertreten* (performative). We thus see, in *A Critique of Postcolonial Reason*, a significant development of strategy vis-à-vis representation. With parabasis, it is no longer merely understood as exposure, but also performed as disruption.

The implications of this move are revealed even more profoundly when this disruptive 'permanent parabasis' is set out in the Appendix to *A Critique of Postcolonial Reason* as the 'setting to work of deconstruction'; the 'setting-to-work of deconstruction without reserve' (*CPR* 430). Readers of the Appendix are in a position to re-read the earlier exposition on representation in Marx; inscribing tragedy as farce, *The Eighteenth Brumaire* operates a parabasis, standing aside from parliamentary paternalism, and stands forth as a setting to work of deconstruction. The Appendix makes plain how high the stakes are when the deconstruction that is set to work exceeds theoretical formalization and the theoretical practice of the academy. Described in terms of de Man's definition of irony, this deconstruction without reserve is 'permanent parabasis or sustained interruption from a source relating "otherwise" (*allegorein* = speaking otherwise) to the continuous unfolding of the main system of meaning – both the formalization of deconstruction and, on another level of abstraction, the logic of global development' (*CPR* 430). This parabasis is dramatized as the shifting place for a 'reader', and for 'reading-otherwise', which increasingly characterizes the book in the 'Culture' chapter, as its writer 'circulates' (*CPR* 377), cutting rapidly from one occasion to the next. Reading, in this case, is not reading in the narrow sense. What Spivak refers to as 'training in a literary habit of reading the world' or 'transnational literacy' (*CPR* xii, 357) is meant for an implied reader on an analogy with factory workers as the implied readers of Marx's *Capital*, who are called upon to 'rethink themselves as agents of production, not as victims of capitalism' (*CPR* 357). Spivak's implied readers, however, are not factory workers, but 'the hyphenated Americans belonging loosely to the . . . groups [comprising of Eurocentric migrants, and seekers of political asylum]', who by a fractured analogy with Marx, 'might rethink themselves as *possible* agents of exploitation, not its victims'. '[T]hen', Spivak continues, 'the idea that the nation-state that they now call home gives "aid" to the nation-state that they still call culture, in order to consolidate the new unification for international capital, might lead to what I call "transnational literacy" ' (*CPR* 357).

I explore in my next chapter the implications of this analysis in Spivak's writings on feminism. In the meantime I pursue further how 'Can the Subaltern Speak?' represents a reading of Marx after Derrida. With a view to sketching some of the larger implications relating to deconstruction and Marxism, I conclude with some questions.

Were this speaking- and reading-otherwise, this 'setting-to-work of deconstruction without reserve', to be characterized as 'a constant pushing away – a differing and a deferral – of the *capital*-ist harnessing of the *social* productivity of capital' (*CPR* 430), would Marxism itself, particularly as it envisions the transition from capitalism to socialism, not also be describable as a setting to work of deconstruction?[9] The short answer for Spivak would be yes, as several remarks in *A Critique of Postcolonial Reason* indicate (*CPR* 67 and *passim*). The reasoning behind the yes is, however, worth a brief elaboration. In classical Marxist terms, the difference between capitalism and socialism is that, although they feature the socialization of production as a common element, with capitalism the surplus yielded by that production is privately appropriated while with socialism it is socially distributed. Spivak can be read as rephrasing these classical terms for her implied reader: the relatively privileged metropolitan double of the Native Informant; the NI lately redone as New Immigrant in a financialized global economy. In the context of addressing that reader, the setting to work of deconstruction without reserve can be understood as an exposure and active disrupting of the representation (*Darstellung*) of socialized capital as capital*ist*; consequently, the representation (*Vertretung*) of the general will as being *for* capital*ism*. As the final pages of the 'History' chapter, and accompanying footnote to Lenin's *Imperialism* indicate, bringing us nearer to the vanishing present of the book's subtitle, the latest stage of capitalism is 'imperialism'. At that point it is, ultimately, a matter of global financialization constructing a general will in the credit-baited rural woman, whose labour has been not only been intensively socialized (*CPR* 68) but is in effect also bonded labour paying off interest on loan capital.[10] In the construction of this general will, 'Bhubaneswari's eldest sister's eldest daughter's eldest daughter's eldest daughter . . . a new U.S. immigrant' (*CPR* 310) is, roughly speaking, the exemplary collaborative agent. As the book's implied reader, the New Immigrant, who is asked to view herself as a possible agent of exploitation, is called upon to draw back from collaboration in the process. This is where cultural politics is pivotal, and the 'Culture' chapter suggests practices. The New Immigrant, or, more precisely, her daughter or granddaughter, is enjoined to develop 'transnational literacy'. Critically articulating the two senses of representation in play, this transnational literacy would lead to an exposure of US multiculturalism's representation (*Darstellung*) of immigrants' countries of origin as 'repositories for cultural nostalgia', and an accompanying active work at maximizing the meaningful representation in civil society (*Vertretung*) of rural women in the South. Whereas multiculturalism works to win the consent of these women for transnational capitalism and to construct in them a general will for globalization, Spivak advocates turning capitalist accumulation toward social redistribution when she points out that '[t]he possibility of persistently redirecting accumulation into social redistribution can be within their reach if they join the globe-girdling Social Movements in the South through the entry point of their own countries of origin' (*CPR* 397–402). Set out in these terms, it becomes plain how *A Critique of Postcolonial Reason* rewrites Marxism as a setting to work of deconstruction: the transnationally literate New Immigrant works, beginning with cultural politics but not ending there, to push away, to differ and defer, the capitalist harnessing of the social productivity of capital. Exposing the interested representation (*Darstellung*) of culture, she does so in the name of the representation (*Vertretung*) of the woman of the South. The latter, her phantasmatic double, is the NI as Native Informant, the (im)possible figure in the name of whom the parabasis is operated. Although, in these terms, the Native Informant occupies a limit, and is a check upon vanguardism, the goal of this parabasis remains an orthodox one: not to preserve subalternity, but, without ignoring the attendant complicities, to bring the subaltern into parliamentary representation (*CPR* 309–10).[11]

From this arises a question: if Spivak's book is '*Capital*' for implied readers in middle-management, corporate or academic, has it given up the project for socialism from below? On the one hand, by defining its implied reader the way it does, *A Critique of Postcolonial Reason* takes up the more limited project of encouraging the upwardly mobile metropolitan migrant to 'join' in solidarity with global movements. This is, however, only part of the picture. First of all, there is localized 'counter-globalist or alternative-development activism' which operates the parabasis to 'the logic of global development' (*CPR* 429). But there is another dimension. If the book is declaredly written for the metropolitan migrant, it also sets out another 'literacy', which is the essential counterpart to that feasible in the metropole, and in which the New Immigrant meets a limit:

The figure of the New Immigrant has a radical limit: those who have stayed in place for more than thirty thousand years. We need not value the limit for itself, but we must take it into account. Is there an alternative vision of the human here? The tempo of learning to learn from this immensely slow temporizing will not only take us clear out of diasporas, but will also yield no answers or conclusions readily. Let this stand as the name of the other of the question of diaspora. That question, so taken for granted these days as the historically necessary ground of resistance, marks the forgetting of this name. Friday? (*CPR* 402)

Friday, the character from Coetzee's novel *Foe*, is one figure of the limit, a figure in the margin. Friday has no tongue, and does not speak. Although the limit, such non-speaking, need not be valued for itself,[12] it is one version of the alterity which makes Marxism, in Spivak's rewriting, a setting to work of deconstruction.

I proposed in Chapter 1 how the specific textuality of colonialism and postcoloniality produces the impossible perspective/figure of the Native Informant who operates the parabasis (*CPR* 37) necessary for a counter-inscription. What is striking, however, especially as one reads the Appendix and its account of the development of Derrida's thinking from *différance* and 'guarding the question' to a 'call to the wholly other' (*CPR* 425), is how *A Critique of Postcolonial Reason* insists upon a place for alterity, for responsibility in Marxism (as the setting to work of deconstruction): 'the splitting off of socialism from capitalism is perceived as grounded in the prior economy between self-preservation and the call of the other' (*CPR* 430). To once again impossibly distil a reading into a single question: does the reframing work done by *A Critique of Postcolonial Reason* suggest that a Marxist or socialist ethics is possible, if the system is persistently exceeded, and/or disrupted, by the projection (*Darstellung*) of the figure of the other which, being prior to the self, is also the figure for whom one is always already a proxy (*Vertretung*)? If it does, the permanent parabasis of *darstellen* and *vertreten* set out and pursued in 'Can the Subaltern Speak?' and *A Critique of Postcolonial Reason* would be another formulation of reading-otherwise as response to the call of the wholly other. And this would, in turn, be the alterity in the name of which what Spivak calls 'a constant pushing away – a differing and a deferral – of the *capital*-ist harnessing of the *social* productivity of capital' (*CPR* 430) takes place.

Defective for capitalism

Spivak enters into these difficult questions in a new and intriguing way in *Imperatives to Re-imagine the Planet* (1999) and 'From Haverstock Hill Flat to U.S. Classroom, What's Left of Theory?' (2000). At the end of 'Can the Subaltern Speak?', as reframed in *A Critique of Postcolonial Reason*, Spivak turns to finance capital, and the role of the Native Informant/ New Immigrant in credit-baiting and other activities. What implications does this turn have for Spivak's careful unpacking of the Marxian text on labour power, industrial capital and the transition from capitalism to socialism? Does Spivak's analysis of finance capital have any bearing on this transition?

These are important questions for Marxists writing today. In *The New Imperialism*, David Harvey, like a number of his predecessors, sees a crisis of overaccumulation in the advanced capitalist economies that leads to investment for higher returns in the periphery – including what he calls 'accumulation by dispossession', in such forms as the devaluation and privatization of state assets. This is a contemporary form of what Marx termed 'primitive accumulation'. Answers are not easy to find. Harvey's solution is to embrace the anti-globalization movement in its diversity, but without engaging in 'nostalgia for what has been lost' (*New Imperialism* 178). Spivak's analysis of the current conjuncture takes a slightly different, or at least more micrological, approach. On the one hand, her analysis of parliamentary representation in 'Can the Subaltern Speak?' anticipates her later preoccupation with the subaltern as citizen and the idea of democracy from below (see 'A Dialogue on Democracy'). In the context of credit-baiting and the creation of a general will for globalization, the vote can be a brake – *perhaps*, since the voter in the rural South is constantly manipulated by electoral propaganda – as Medovoi and others, to Spivak's satisfaction (*CPR* 309–10), point out when they analyse Nicaraguan elections in 'Can the Subaltern Vote?' When the coercively rearranged desires of the voter diverge from his or her interests, permanent parabasis grows more complicated.

A more radical idea is mooted in Spivak's most recent writings. As I discussed in Chapter 1, in 'Righting Wrongs' Spivak advocates the suturing of ethical systems 'defective for capitalism' so that they can supplement the logic of capital accumulation, and turn capitalism toward socialism. This idea is set out in more detail in 'From Haverstock Hill Flat to U.S. Classroom, What's Left of Theory?' and in *Imperatives to Re-imagine the Planet*, where it is linked to finance capital, globalization and what Spivak calls the 'spectralization of the rural'.

After concluding her account of how, when one reads the key passages on use value in *Capital*, volume one, 'Marx is theorizing and Engels is running interference, with the intention of making things clearer for the implied working-class reader' ('From Haverstock Hill' 3), Spivak writes that today:

> the untrammeled power of the abstract – financialization of the globe – economically and ideologically managed from within capital – world trade – cannot be managed – supplemented – by opposing perspectives from within. Today Marx's ghost needs stronger offerings than Human Rights with economics worked in, or the open-ended messianicity of the future anterior, or even 'responsibility' (choice or being-called) in the Western tradition. The need is to turn toward ethical practices – care of others as care of the self – that were '*defective* for capitalism.' Marx must be turned around to those who lost in the capitalist competition again and again; in order to turn this ferociously powerful form of capital around to the social. ('From Haverstock Hill' 7)

The idea of ethical practices 'defective for capitalism', attributed to Foucault's late writings, ought perhaps to be unpacked in a literal way. Etymologically, this Latinate word *defect* may be analysed as combining the prefix *de-* with the root *facere*, meaning to make or to do. The word *defeat* has the same root. 'Defective', therefore, can mean both lacking in something, and, more literally, an un-doing of something. Both of these senses appear to be in play for Spivak when she outlines in more detail the implications of these ethical practices.

One of the problems with invoking these practices is that, as Spivak observes, drawing on Mahmood Mamdani's analysis of the colonial codification of African 'customary law' in *Citizen and Subject*, 'there may be nothing (authentic) left with which to associate labor in the interest of the social' ('From Haverstock Hill' 10). More precisely, '[t]he structural outlines of responsibility-based cultural practices begin to atrophy into residual scaffolding as industrial capitalist imperialisms impose the dominant structures, whose motor is rights-based' ('From Haverstock Hill' 12). Another problem is that, as Spivak notes in a parenthesis, 'as soon as a culture systematizes responsibility, the contingency of "responsibility" begins to atrophy even without the intervention of an "alien" dominant' ('From Haverstock Hill' 12). This is, Spivak argues, how 'these systems, reactive to colonial domination of the males, often turn increasingly gender-compromised', and in which culturalism may be 'way[s] of keeping women backward' ('From Haverstock Hill' 10, 16).

Despite these problems, Spivak attends to the prayer to be haunted and the ghost dance. In a long passage quoted from *Imperatives to Re-imagine the Planet* – like 'From Haverstock Hill Flat', originally a lecture delivered in 1997 – she suggests that:

> without an education into a drastic epistemic transformation, capital – industrial and finance – cannot be persistently checked and turned around to the interest of the social. I am further arguing that this social practice of responsibility based on an imperative imagined as intended from alterity . . . cannot today be related to any named grounding. . . . I am further suggesting that, rather than honoring the historical happenstance, that the rational machine of capital logic required the destruction of this understanding of the individual, and thus dismiss it as 'pre-capitalist,' we might imagine it animating and inspiriting the abstract structures of democratic guarantees, which are indeed a great good. ('From Haverstock Hill' 14–15)

Since these practices of responsibility are atrophied, as Spivak writes in 'Righting Wrongs', they have to be 'reinvent[ed]' and 'reconstellat[ed] . . . into the abstractions of the democratic structures of civil society' ('From Haverstock Hill' 15, 17).

In the process, there will be a reciprocal transformation. The idea of 'civil society', related to the *city*, will, in the light of the functioning of contemporary capital, have to change. The countryside is, tacitly, the space where the ethical practices abide. With globalization, however, comes the 'spectralization of the rural' ('From Haverstock Hill' 27). This is linked, in Spivak's thinking, to the shift to finance capital.

In a key passage, Spivak relocates the entire complex of her reading of *Capital*:

> After the European recession of the 1870s, Lenin already knew that the major theater of spectralization had shifted to commercial capital. Already spectralized labor-power, use-value in capital accumulation, had lost its unique power to socialize capital as agent of production. One of the longest chapters in Lenin's book *Imperialism* is entitled 'Banks.' He could not envisage a World Bank yet. ('From Haverstock Hill' 27)

If use-value and labour power have lost their (unique) power, that would also mean, in Spivak's thinking, that the agent of labour power – namely, the worker – has lost his or her (unique) power to turn capital toward the social. This is a tremendous shift of gravity, given Spivak's meticulous unpicking of the Marxian text. Who is the agent now? *Capital* will no longer provide the answers that she needs. Reading the world remains her only solution. In *A Critique of Postcolonial Reason* it appeared to be the NI as New Immigrant and facilitator for global finance. In 'From Haverstock Hill Flat' it is not entirely clear. A clue lies in the fact that the rural is accessed directly by finance capital ('From Haverstock Hill' 29; cf. *CPR* ix). That would not exclude the NI as facilitator. But – to use a phrase often used by Spivak – at the other side of the global division of labour, the agent must needs be different. The name given by Spivak to this agent is the Aboriginal. Faced with biopiracy and credit-baiting, what might this agent do? There are only the most cryptic of hints as, again, resistance is viewed as ironic 'permanent parabasis':

> In [finance capital's] coding through world trade . . . it invokes land and the embodied female subject. And it is here that the always partially spectralized 'rural' confronts the forces of the global face-to-face. . . . The time of seed and DNA is not 'real' or 'local' time, it is irrelevant to subject-speak, open only to an open place of agency. The definition of the 'subaltern' is now being rewritten. It is the group that, although or perhaps because, cut off from ordinary lines of mobility, is being touched directly by global telecommunication: the spectrality of indigenous knowledge, the databasing of DNA-patenting of the most remote groups, the credit-baiting of the poorest rural women. ('From Haverstock Hill' 30–3).

If Spivak's allusions to 'resistance networks' as the actors in the parabasis in question – and '[t]riumphant global finance capital/world trade can only be resisted with irony' ('From Haverstock Hill' 33) – are short on detail, it may because the 'literary critic, "reading" the social text' ('From Haverstock Hill' 31) is presented as *following* what these actors do. It is in the texts discussed at the end of Chapter 1, however, that the literary critic takes the lead, proposing rural literacy and teacher training as definite ways of performing this parabasis. As is clear from 'Righting Wrongs', this involves a tremendous risk and leap of faith – as ethical practices defective for capitalism are repaired, activated and reconstellated with the structures of democracy. So far everything that Spivak has written in this area is provisional.[13] In the next chapter I enter into the implications for feminism of Spivak's proposals for reading the world, hinted at in *A Critique of Postcolonial Reason* by its references to credit-baiting, and in 'From Haverstock Hill Flat' by references to a female subject that is embodied.

Notes

1 See, for, example, Michael Ryan's *Marxism and Deconstruction: A Critical Articulation* (1982). Derrida lists several other names in *Specters* (184–5n9).

2 A representative sampling of English-language responses is the 1999 collection, edited by Michael Sprinker, *Ghostly Demarcations: A Symposium on Jacques Derrida's* Specters of Marx.

3 See Derrida, 'Marx & Sons' 222–3.

4 In 'Il faut s'y prendre en s'en prenant à elles', Spivak's contribution to *Les fins de l'homme*, only the first sentence up until the comma appears.

5 Although the 1987 version of 'Speculation on Reading Marx' includes passages from 'Scattered Speculations', I take it, originally published in 1983 as 'Marx after Derrida', to be the earlier of the two essays.

6 For an account of the Marxist Literary Group and the conference, see Homer, 'A Short History'.

7 See 'Speculation on Reading Marx' 35; 'Scattered Speculations on the Question of Value' (*IOW* 155–9).

8 This is the caution ignored by Benita Parry when she criticizes Spivak for 'giv[ing] no speaking part to the colonized, effectively writing out the evidence of native agency recorded in India's 200 year struggle against British conquest and the Raj' ('Problems' 35). For Spivak's response to Parry, see *CPR* 190–1.

9 For another critical articulation of Marxism and deconstruction, see the discussion of Fredric Jameson on postmodernism at the beginning of the 'Culture' chapter (*CPR* 312–36).

10 Spivak links bonded labour and the 'financialization of the globe' in her reading of Mahasweta Devi's story 'Douloti', in *Outside in the Teaching Machine* (*OTM* 95). For an excellent reading of *A Critique of Postcolonial Reason* in terms of finance capital and credit-baiting, see Baucom, 'Cryptic, Withheld, Singular' (413–17).

11 '[W]orking *for* the subaltern is precisely to bring them, *not* through cultural benevolence, but through extra-academic work, into the circuit of parliamentary democracy. . . . even as we try to keep them alive, we cannot forget that working *for* the subaltern *means* the subaltern's insertion into citizenship, whatever that might mean, and thus the undoing of subaltern space' (*Spivak Reader* 307).

12 As Baucom and Al-Kassim have noted, insisting upon the Native Informant as a limit is one of the central gestures of *A Critique of Postcolonial Reason*. It is crucial also to note, though, that, in cultural politics and in politics more

generally, when representation (as *Darstellung* and as *Vertretung*) is contested, this limit is transgressed, even if it is only through a 'responsible and minimal identitarianism' (*CPR* 156n). Hallward's critique of Spivak's insistence on this limit (*Absolutely Postcolonial* 27–35) does not, to my mind, acknowledge that Spivak conceives of such an insistence as a disruption of value-coding.

13 See also her remarks on *dvaita* as the interruption of *advaita* in 'Moving Devi' (124, 127).

Chapter 4

Feminism Internationalized

Spivak's writing on feminism ranges widely. After some initial forays into literary criticism and literary theory – in quest of 'feminist readings' of Dante, Yeats and other writers (*IOW* 15–76) – a clearer, more definitive tendency establishes itself. One notices a series of departures, as Spivak, whose early feminist criticism follows the patterns of the subdiscipline as it evolved among deconstructionist and psychoanalytic critics in the United States, begins to define herself against metropolitan feminism and its unquestioned assumptions and agendas. Producing a rupture between Western and Third World feminism, between French and international feminism, this questioning has not ceased.

Another line of questioning, to be traced in its earliest form to a few remarks in essays of the original departure, effects another – one which, I will argue, is the more telling of the two, and represents the more singular contribution of Spivak to feminist theory, commentary and cultural critique – to reading the world as a feminist. That second path of questioning repeats the first by bringing about a division in what had, at first, been represented as a unit. If, in the first instance, that unit was an undifferentiated feminism or 'woman', and Spivak's move was to differentiate between Western or French feminism and Third World women and international feminism, in this instance, the critical term itself undergoes critique.

From the beginning, there are intimations of the element that would, in time, become dominant: the split within the term Third World woman, later phrased as a complicity in the agendas of metropolitan feminism as they are implicated in colonialism, neocolonialism and globalization. When 'Can the Subaltern Speak?' is revised for inclusion in *A Critique of Postcolonial Reason*, so as to foreground the female NI (New Immigrant/Native Informant) as agent of global capital, and to point to the differential position of women in the financialization of the globe, we can see this as a culmination of a process of interrogation begun much earlier. In the original version of 'Can the Subaltern Speak?' we find a powerful critique of the collaboration of colonial subjects in the codification of colonial power and then, at the end of that essay, the dramatic coda about the suicide of Bhubaneswari Bhaduri and the stories about it circulated by her female relatives. In the colonial era, the determinations of Hindu law and the prohibition of *sati* by the British represent a male, patriarchal confluence of interests. In a later era, Spivak shows, we can detect a female complicity in the un-speaking of a subject who resisted both colonial power and the interpretations put forward about her death.

This is, however, not the first time that Spivak foregrounds this complicity – and what is remarkable is that, in doing so, from the start, she includes herself, sometimes in cryptic ways, in her critique. This chapter, tracking this inclusion, is, accordingly, divided into four sections. The first two, on her early differings, treat two key texts, 'French Feminism in an International Frame' (1981) and 'Three Women's Texts and a Critique of Imperialism' (1985). They set out, on the one hand, Spivak's critique of Western feminism and feminist individualism, as well as her attempt to bridge the rupture between it and Third World women through the violent figure of clitoridectomy. As I showed in Chapter 2, for Spivak this represents a setting to work of deconstruction. On the other hand, these two sections consider in detail how Spivak makes herself the subject of her critique. Writing in the genre of the familiar essay she interrogates 'privilege' in 'French Feminism in an International Frame', and when she implies elsewhere that *Jane Eyre* was a book she read as a child, she may be implying a formative individualist identification with the novel's protagonist.[1] The third section deals with Spivak's elaboration, in the 1980s, of a self-implicating account of the formation of the colonial and postcolonial subject – which, in contrast to accounts by Frantz Fanon and Ngũgĩ wa Thiong'o of the comprador class, puts gender at the centre. In this section, I go on to examine Spivak's analysis of the international division of labour along with her position of privilege in the United States. The latter, as it changes with the 'vanishing present', becomes exemplary for reading the world, for what she began, in the mid-1990s, to call 'transnational literacy' (see 'Teaching for the Times'), and which parallels the work of other contemporary feminist analysts such as Maria Mies, and has influenced the work of others – whose 'critical endeavour to situate women's social location in a transnational framework of political, economic and social relationships is one of the most important legacies of Spivak's thought' (Morton, *Gayatri Chakravorty Spivak* 139). In the final section, I track an evolution in Spivak's thinking in the 1990s and 2000s that unites her critique of subject-formation and of implication in transnational capital in confrontation with finance capital and the forms that it takes in the global South: credit-baiting, and the role of 'universal feminism' and of the metropolitan migrant/middle-class female postcolonial (NI) in creating a 'general will for globalization'.

French feminism

In 'French Feminism in an International Frame', first published in a 1981 special issue of *Yale French Studies* entitled 'Feminist Readings: French Texts/American Contexts', Spivak outlines her feminist intellectual trajectory. The essay begins with an anecdote about '[a] young Sudanese woman in the Faculty of Sociology at a Saudi Arabian University', who says that she has 'written a structural functionalist dissertation on female circumcision in the Sudan'. This surprises Spivak because it implies 'applaud[ing] a system – in this case sexual – because it functions'; it also, however, brings home to her her own capture, as an emigrant academic, in a 'web of information retrieval' about 'so-called Third World women' (*IOW* 134–5):

> In my Sudanese colleague's research I found an allegory for my own ideological victimage:
>   The 'choice' of English Honors by an upper-class young woman in the Calcutta of the fifties was itself highly overdetermined. Becoming a professor of English in the U.S. fitted in with the 'brain drain.' In due course, a commitment to feminism was the best of a collection of accessible scenarios. The morphology of a feminist theoretical practice came clear through Jacques Derrida's critique of phallocentrism and Luce Irigaray's reading of Freud. (The stumbling 'choice' of French avant-garde criticism by an undistinguished Ivy League Ph.D. working in the Midwest is itself not without ideology-critical interest.) Predictably, I began by identifying 'female academic' and feminism as such. Gradually I found that there was indeed an area of feminist scholarship in the U.S. that was called 'International Feminism': the arena usually defined as feminism in England, France, West Germany, Italy, and that part of the Third World most easily accessible to American interests: Latin America. When one attempted to think of so-called Third World women in a broader scope, one found oneself caught,

as my Sudanese colleague was caught and held by Structural Functionalism, in a web of information retrieval inspired at best by: 'what can I do *for* them?' (*IOW* 134–5)

Here, as elsewhere in Spivak, 'allegory' is a keyword if we read it etymologically as a speaking-otherwise. The source of an 'allegory', the expatriate Sudanese scholar is an uncanny double, an encounter with whom leads her to think and write her life otherwise. The resulting curriculum vitae takes stock of decisions hitherto taken and recognizes influences. It also lays several tracks for subsequent departures.

Engaging in feminist consciousness-raising along its classical lines, Spivak rethinks her privilege as a female academic in the United States as 'ideological victimage', and appeals to colleagues to do likewise. The envisaged change of consciousness is of immense import: the subject is made in history; 'highly overdetermined' in my 'choices', I am not history's source. Unless a commitment to feminism is viewed in these terms, there is no chance of learning about, or from, Third World women (see *IOW* 136). This idea is condensed into a slogan: unlearning one's privilege (see, for instance, *Post-Colonial Critic* 30, 42, 57). Because it appeared to license a certain narcissism among Spivak's followers, this slogan is later withdrawn in favour of another: learning to learn from below (see, for example, 'Setting to Work' 165). In the meantime, however, it serves as an indispensable waymark for an itinerary in which subjective self-centeredness will be questioned relentlessly and repeatedly. If privilege is law for oneself (*privi-legium*), to unlearn it is to accept the other as legislator. Over and over, autonomy is supplemented by heteronomy – which is, in any case, its *parergon* or 'frame'.

Her morphology is, as Spivak informs us, deconstructive. She had by this time published her translation of *Of Grammatology* with her influential preface, as well as meticulous discussions of Derrida in 'Revolutions That as Yet Have No Model' and '*Glas*-Piece: A *compte rendu*'. But what is particularly interesting in 'French Feminism in an International Frame' is that, by being implicated in an autobiography written as a coming-to-consciousness and academic transition from 'English' to 'French avant-garde criticism', the deconstructive morphology is itself held up for scrutiny. French feminist texts, Spivak writes, could be a problem, merely reproducing the drive for knowledge of 'West' about 'East', or they could be 'something like a solution – reversing and displacing (if only by juxtaposing "some French texts" and a "certain Calcutta") the ironclad opposition of West and East' (*IOW* 135). Reversal and displacement – the formula for deconstruction given by Derrida in

'Signature Event Context' (329) – thus work at more than one level in Spivak's essay, connecting a reinscription of privilege as victimage with an overturning of a geo-political binary of East and West that overdetermines the placement of the migrant literary theorist.

In all of this, the Third World woman, with whom Spivak does not claim identification, stands as a limit – to knowledge, to any vanguardist politics. Although she will be summoned in Spivak's writings by other names – 'native', 'subaltern', for instance – the limit that she figures becomes a permanent one. 'French Feminism in an International Frame' proceeds to present a second anecdote (one frequently discussed by critics). It is 'an obstinate childhood memory':

> I am walking alone in my grandfather's estate on the Bihar-Bengal border one winter afternoon in 1949. Two ancient washerwomen are washing clothes in the river, beating the clothes on the stones. One accuses the other of poaching on her part of the river. I can still hear the cracked derisive voice of the one accused: 'You fool! Is this your river? The river belongs to the Company!' – the East India Company, from whom India passed to England by the Act for the Better Government of India (1858); England had transferred its charge to an Indian Governor-General in 1947. India would become an independent republic in 1950. For these withered women, the land as soil and water to be used rather than a map to be learned still belonged, as it did one hundred and nineteen years before that date, to the East India Company.
>
> I was precocious enough to know that the remark was incorrect. It has taken me thirty-one years and the experience of confronting a nearly inarticulable question to apprehend that their facts were wrong but the fact was right. The Company does still own the land. (*IOW* 135)

Serving to turn the tables on the confident, know-it-all child, the anecdote motivates a transition from information-retrieval (epistemology) to dialogic interaction (ethics): 'The academic feminist must learn to learn from them, to speak to them, to suspect that their access to the political and sexual scene is not merely to be *corrected* by our superior theory and enlightened compassion' (*IOW* 135). This shift from the epistemological to the ethical, the supplemental disruption of knowing by doing, is, as I have argued above, basic to all of Spivak's subsequent work. In other contexts, this shift is described in terms of the change, in the work of Derrida, from 'guarding the question' to the 'call to the wholly other'. It is remarkable that in 'French Feminism in an International Frame' the alteration that in Derrida's thought Spivak dates to the 1980 conference on 'The Ends of Man' at Cerisy-la-Salle (*CPR* 425)[2] is taking place in a way apparently unanticipated by Derrida as she brings deconstruction to bear on the question of international feminism.

What is even more interesting is that, in Spivak's essay, the turn toward the call of the wholly other takes place by way of a series of figures. That the child in the anecdote is 'alone' is crucial for several reasons. Being the sole witness, her 'obstinate . . . memory' is, strictly speaking, unverifiable. The child is also alone in the sense that, as the story is related, she does not exist for the washerwomen, although they exist for her. She is alone without being alone, the condition in which Biblical tradition tells us that prophets receive their calling. In Spivak's case, although her vocation is entirely secular, such an aloneness without being alone will have been a condition of possibility for her questioning of thirty-one years later. Repetition makes memory, makes it be the first time: 'I can still hear . . . the voice'. This receptive but uncomprehending child, then, is the figure that is the figure for the 'academic feminist' that the child will have become.

These are not the only figures. If the old woman whose direct speech is rendered stands ultimately as a figure of heterogeneity beyond the ken of the native informant, she is remembered to have been heard to speak in a particular way. The style of her question makes her a figure of irony, in the general sense of a parabasis; after the Sudanese woman, the second instance in two pages of allegory as a speaking-otherwise. Although the old woman does not *address* the child, the child is, over-hearing her, addressed by her: called to her, in Derrida's formulation. If the Socrates of Plato's *Apology* is the classical example for the *eiron*, the ironic questioner is the one who, dissembling ignorance, makes non-sense of claims at knowing: 'You fool! Is this your river?' The apparent statement of fact '[t]he river belongs to the Company' contains a cata-chresis. It does not, as the clever child observes, gel with the known facts to say that the East India Company owns the river. What takes her thirty-one years to realize is that the words uttered in the voice that she still hears are couched in a rhetoricity that her immature ear was unready to discern. Confuting a claim to know is, in this context, also a questioning of ownership. A catachresis that runs counter to commonly accepted facts, a figure not a guarantee of presence, the washerwoman's statement does not claim possession of a fact. The dis-possession she articulates applies as much to her as its speaker as to the estate, its owners and its occupants (including Spivak's grandfather, who managed the estate for its owners).[3] There is historical change, but, as Spivak likes to say, every rupture is also a repetition. The governors are really only tenants: English rule and Indian independence are both, so to speak, established on Company land. Spivak uses the catachresis – the unverifiable 'fact [that] was right' although the facts were wrong – to denote a systemic repetition of capital logic that she will emphasize in all of her writings, not only those on feminism, in order to undo the privileged self-possession of the subject that is both the condition of, and a curb to, transformative agency. That subject-agent's necessary supplement is the figure of the wholly other, the one I do not know, but who calls me, and calls me to her, in an uncanny autonomy that is a heteronomy: a being alone that is a not being alone. The same might be said of Spivak's reading of Bhubaneswari Bhaduri at the end of 'Can the Subaltern Speak?'

When Spivak refers to 'a nearly inarticulate question', that question is being relayed through the question asked by the washerwoman. In the immediate context of her essay, however, the question is: 'What is the constituency of an international feminism?' (*IOW* 135). As is well known, Spivak's essay explores the scope and limits of works by French feminist thinkers who were particularly important for the American academics who contributed to the 'Feminist Readings' number of *Yale French Studies* in which 'French Feminism in an International Frame' first appeared. The principal texts discussed by Spivak are Julia Kristeva's *About Chinese Women*, an account of a visit of the *Tel Quel* group to China, and Hélène Cixous's 'Laugh of the Medusa', an essay offering advice to a young writer wanting to publish in Paris. Spivak carefully considers the relationship of Kristeva and Cixous to the literary and philosophical avant-garde. Kristeva is criticized along with those French theorists who reach out to 'all that is not the West', not so much for the sake of the other but in order to question 'the millennially cherished excellences of Western metaphysics: the sovereignty of the subject's intention, the power of predication and so on' (*IOW* 136). 'In spite of their occasional interest in touching the *other* of the West, of metaphysics, of capitalism, their repeated question is obsessively self-centered: if we are not what official history and philosophy say we are, who then are we (not), how are we (not)?' (*IOW* 137). This is the tendency that Spivak refers to in 'Can the Subaltern Speak?' (*CPR* 266) as an employing of the other to consolidate the self. If what drives the representation of Third World women is the search for a political alternative in the West, there is no other-directedness. 'The question of how to speak *to* the "faceless" women of China cannot be asked within such a partisan conflict' (*IOW* 140). By speaking on behalf of an undifferentiated West, Kristeva's book is part of a larger formation of which Spivak herself is struggling free. 'The fact that Kristeva . . . speaks for a generalized West is the "naturalization transformed into privilege" that I compared to my own ideological victimage' (*IOW* 140). Accordingly, Spivak calls upon Kristeva to examine 'her own pre-history in Bulgaria' (*IOW* 140).

Insisting that, when viewed within an international frame, the differences between 'French' and 'Anglo-American' feminism do not run particularly deep, Spivak calls for a 'simultaneous other focus: not merely who am I? but who is the other woman? How am I naming her? How does she name me? Is this part of the problematic I discuss?' (*IOW* 150). This other focus, is, in the Derridian terms that animate Spivak's essay, a reversal (of investigative attention) and a displacement (of knowing/acting centre). It is, of course, easier said than done. So Spivak, this time taking a leaf from the book of the French feminist avant-garde (Cixous, Irigaray and others),[4] again introduces a figure. The figure of clitoridectomy audaciously links 'West' and its 'others', reversing the place-terms, and displacing the privilege of the critique of the discourse of mothering as implicated in patriarchal ideology of womanhood as reproduction. 'The arena of research here', Spivak insists, however, 'is not merely remote and primitive societies' (*IOW* 151). The lesson that Spivak has learned is from *within* French feminism's 'description of women's pleasure' (*IOW* 150), and its insistence on the clitoris, which, although it 'escapes reproductive framing', is effaced 'as the signifier of the sexed subject' (*IOW* 151). 'Investigation of the effacement of the clitoris – where clitoridectomy is a metonym for women's definition as "legal object as subject of reproduction" – would persistently seek to de-normalize uterine social organization' (*IOW* 152). The 'best gift of French feminism' is a writing that will 'straddle and undo the ideological-material opposition'. When Spivak concludes with the idea that 'here is a theme that can liberate my colleague from Sudan, and a theme the old washerwoman by the river would understand', there is a certain utopianism, 'a sense of our common yet history-specific lot' (*IOW* 153). While one can question the attribution of the particular idea to the washerwoman – unless one reads her view of the river as Company property as similarly straddling and undoing the ideological–material opposition, and even then is it really a 'talking to' her? – the return in closing to the Sudanese academic, Spivak's uncanny allegorizing double, makes the understanding in question that of Spivak herself. As Spivak later asks, '[i]f the non-"European" feminine is ungeneralizable as woman, socio-culturally constructed or otherwise, what is the validity of Eurocentric feminism?' ('Feminist Literary Criticism' 613). The break that the feminist makes cannot be the self-centred and self-consolidating political tourism of *Tel Quel*; it must come from within as it reaches out. The faultline must traverse self as well as other.

Individualism

With a few key remarks in 'Three Women's Texts and a Critique of Imperialism' (1985) Spivak's critique of Western feminism turns from French philosophy and literature towards the specific English intellectual and political traditions that helped to shape her early life. If, in 'French Feminism in an International Frame', French thought ruptures a putative continuity in the study and teaching of 'English' literature, 'Three Women's Texts' returns to an earlier subject-formation and to what it continues to mean despite that ensuing rupture.

Although 'Three Women's Texts' is primarily a work of literary criticism, it is noteworthy beyond its readings in that in it Spivak tacitly presents herself not simply as a victim of British cultural imperialism – an Indian university student whose choice of 'English' is 'highly overdetermined' – but as a colonial, or postcolonial subject, complicit as agent in a feminist mission (activist, reforming, even civilizing) that she exposes and criticizes in her discussion of novels by Charlotte Brontë, Jean Rhys and Mary Shelley.[5] Spivak's target is not only the feminism of the academy, but the far larger formation of individualism – what C.B. MacPherson termed possessive individualism. This formation, Spivak proposes, has underwritten feminism in the Anglo-American and European world since the nineteenth century: 'feminism within the social relations and institutions of the metropolis has something like a relationship with the fight for individualism in the upwardly class-mobile bourgeois class politics of the European nineteenth century' (*CPR* 147–8).

The link between feminist individualism, benevolent sisterhood and imperialist power is no mere figment of the theorist's imagination. That this collaboration flourishes and is energetically advocated *today* is no better exemplified than by Camille Paglia, who writes in a forum on 'American Gender Studies Today' (1999), also contributed to by Spivak, that:

> [t]here are . . . two primary spheres of future action: first, basic civil rights and educational opportunity must be secured *for* Third World women; second, the education and training of western women must

be better designed to prepare them for leadership positions in business and politics. . . . Military history, not feminist theory, is required: without an understanding of war, few women will ever be entrusted with topmost positions in government. (213; my emphasis)

That Paglia's point is borne out by the fact that in the United States, as at time of writing, geo-political strategist Condoleezza Rice is Secretary of State, and Hillary Rodham Clinton busies herself on the Senate Armed Services Committee in an effort to burnish her credentials as a future Presidential candidate, only goes to show how thoroughgoing the implications are. One might add that, in uniting sovereignty of the self and of the nation/empire, to include the waging of war as 'commander-in-chief', Paglia's individualism includes the prerogative to put to death that, according to Derrida (see 'Autoimmunity' 124) and others, is a sine qua non of Western thinking of sovereignty.

In literary works, the sovereign prerogative to kill may be displaced, and represented as the voluntary dying of the other. Spivak's reading of Brontë's *Jane Eyre*, a novel that she read as a child ('Setting to Work' 171), is that the Other woman must destroy herself in order for the Englishwoman to realize herself as individual and individualist. Spivak daringly links this to *sati* in India – the final act of the 'good wife'. In Brontë's novel, Bertha Mason burns herself up as she sets the *domus* on fire, 'so that Jane Eyre can become the feminist individualist heroine of British fiction' (*CPR* 127). In *Wide Sargasso Sea* (1966), however, Jean Rhys rewrites Brontë to have Antoinette, the mad Creole bride that Rochester likes to call Bertha, dream of burning the house down, but the novel ends, in indeterminate fashion, with her leaving her forced seclusion with a candle and the words 'Now at last I know why I was brought here and what I have to do' (quoted in *CPR* 127). Refusing to have her complete the script of self-immolation, Rhys's book 'critique[s] the axiomatics of imperialism in substance and rhetoric. . . . Rhys sees to it that the woman from the colonies is not sacrificed as an insane animal for her sister's consolation' (*CPR* 115, 127).[6]

Spivak summarizes the implications of her reading:

> what is at stake, for feminist individualism in the age of imperialism, is precisely the making of human beings, the constitution and 'interpellation' of the subject not only as individual but as 'individualist.' This stake is represented in two registers: childrearing and soul-making. The first is domestic-society-through-sexual-reproduction cathected as 'companionate love'; the second is the

imperialist project cathected as civil-society-through-social-mission. As the female individualist, not-quite-not-male, articulates herself in shifting relationship to what is at stake, the 'native subaltern female' (*within* discourse, *as* a signifier) is excluded from any share in this emerging norm' (*CPR* 116–17).

In the original version of the essay, 'native subaltern female' read 'native female' ('Three Women's Texts' 245).[7] The interpolation of 'subaltern' in *A Critique of Postcolonial Reason* is a telling one. By recognizing class differentiation within the entity 'native women', it transforms the colonial subject from unqualified victim into qualified victimizer. A term originally drawn from Keats, soul-making is Spivak's shorthand for Matthew Arnold's class-mobile project for literary studies, which was exported to and tested in the colonies (see also 'Burden of English'). A footnote in *A Critique* specifies that '[t]he subaltern . . . is seen over against the emergent bourgeoisie of the colonies, whose share in female emancipation is another story' (*CPR* 117n). This revision is critically self-implicating. Indian women of Spivak's social class, at least of her time, are not the victims in question – although, as she underlines, in the early nineteenth century, upper-class Indian women are not yet interpellated as the individualists that they would be a hundred years later (*CPR* 131). They are, in the sense applicable to Bhubaneswari Bhaduri specified at the end of 'Can the Subaltern Speak?', subaltern. Yet, despite the revision, the rhetorical power of the essay in both of its versions may ultimately depend on the availability of the substitute-figure of the 'native woman' for the essayist-I presenting herself as Native Informant. The revision does what it can to push away this abyss of (dis)identification, not quite (not) implicating the I in the critique of individualism. Increasingly, though, in texts after 1985, and especially in *A Critique of Postcolonial Reason* and after, this figurative substitution is questioned, as the politics of 'national origin validation' in US multiculturalism is debunked, and the privilege of the postcolonial female subject is relentlessly exposed.

The colonial and postcolonial subject in the international division of labour

Semantically, the word 'postcolonial' can mean two things. If, in the parlance of postcolonial studies, to which Spivak has made a singular contribution, it generally refers to the period *after decolonization*, it may also be understood as referring to the period *after colonization*. It is productive, I propose, to take it in the latter sense when considering Spivak's account of subject-formation – in which, although a neocolonial working-class subject is produced in a different way, the older subject continues to be produced as that of bourgeois nationalism.[8]

Hardly anybody will dispute that the most influential critiques of colonial subject-formation are male-centred. This applies to those written from a psychoanalytic as well as a Marxist perspective. Apart from his laceration of Mayotte Capécia's *Je suis martiniquaise* in *Black Skin, White Masks* (1952), which shows how the author is in love with 'whiteness' (42), the exemplary figure of Frantz Fanon's analysis of the internalization of racism and what, in a coinage of his own, he terms its 'epidermalization', is male. When the Parisian child exclaims 'Look, a Negro!', it is a man who has been caught in the gaze; it is his 'corporeal schema' that has been shattered into a thousand pieces (*Black Skin* 111–12). This applies also when it is a question of learning French (*Black Skin* 17ff). Perhaps the most sustained Marxist account of the cultural politics of colonialism and neo-colonialism today is that of Kenyan author Ngũgĩ wa Thiong'o. In *Detained: A Writer's Prison Diary* (1981) and *Decolonising the Mind* (1986) he exposes how the Kenyan national bourgeoisie operates as a comprador class of middlemen between international capitalism and local resources and markets. Ngũgĩ combines materialist analysis with a psychology of colonization. Members of this privileged class, he argues, are not only economically self-interested to the detriment of their compatriots, but have so deeply imbibed the norms of English-language education and its cultural baggage that they have actually begun to identify not as Africans but as Europeans. The fact that the Kenyan state supports shows like *Jesus Christ Superstar*, but suppresses a grassroots Gĩkũyũ theatre initiative in which Ngũgĩ is involved, and puts him in prison for a year without trial because of it, is proof that the processes he describes are real.

In *Decolonising the Mind*, a series of familiar essays on the language of African fiction, drama and poetry, Ngũgĩ traces his own evolution from Anglophone writing to a series of experiments in the vernacular. Like Fanon, he does not do much to analyse the gendered dynamics of colonial and postcolonial subject-formation. Although Spivak does not discuss *colonial* subject-formation in much detail, the remarks that she makes on the topic make it a pivotal moment in her writings on feminism. As we have seen, from the beginning, with the 'upper-class young woman' in 'French Feminism in an International Frame', Spivak, like Ngũgĩ, has made her own formation the point of entry into, and a didactic frame for, systemic questions.

Spivak's early essays on feminism establish a template that will be progressively adapted in subsequent work. This template comprises two axes. The first is *systemic*, and characterizes world capitalism in its various historical stages: colonialism, imperialism, neo-colonialism, transnationalization, globalization, financialization and so forth. If the first two are associated with Marx and Lenin respectively, and neo-colonialism is the focus of Fanon and Ngũgĩ, Spivak's special contribution is to an analysis of its later forms. The second axis is *subjective*: the formation of the subject and its agency within the system, and at odds with it, typifies Spivak's work.[9] As I noted in my discussion of *A Critique of Postcolonial Reason* in Chapter 1, the colonial subject slides into the postcolonial subject, and the NI of various kinds. Spivak stages herself as each of these figures. Correspondingly, the 'subaltern' is figured as the limit to this subjectification. Supplementing her Marxist template, Spivak employs the concept of subject-position, which she draws from Foucault's *Archaeology of Knowledge*, and adapts psychoanalysis in various ways – for instance, as I discuss in Chapter 5, when she devises the concept of 'regulative psychobiography' and employs it to make sense of Bhubaneswari Bhaduri's life and death (*CPR* 298, 307).

Spivak's most detailed account of the colonial subject and its relation to feminism is found in 'The Political Economy of Women as Seen by a Literary Critic' (1989). There it is contrasted with the production of subjects within the neo-colonial international division of labour:

> In the great age of territorial imperialism, a certain effort at settling the country to make capital flow and thus to facilitate transportation as well as to codify the law and regularize education, was necessary. Thus the social mission-aspect of imperialism took on an ideological hold that for some people became its central task and justification. With this came the training into consumerism 'introducing imperceptibly a gradual improvement in the habits and manners of the people,' to quote an early 19th-century document of the East India Company. . . .
>
> Thus a new code of law, a new system of education, and a new perception of needs operated the epistemic violence – violently changing the shape of the mind and the person – which produced the old colonial subject who had a chance to enter the struggle for individualism.

This elaborate constitution of the subject is not necessary under international subcontracting in post-modern or electronic capitalism. No legal structure need be laid down for the army of 'permanent casuals,' only the circumventing of rudimentary labor and safety regulations is on the agenda. No consistent training into consumerism is any longer needed. The industries can move on. The markets are elsewhere. (224)

Spivak thus recognizes the processes of subject-formation through education, legal codification and training in consumption that, advocated in Thomas Babington Macaulay's 'Minute on Indian Education' (1835) (see *CPR* 268), are the main concern of Fanon, Ngũgĩ and others. Macaulay saw the emergence, through English-style education, of a mediator class of interpreters. Elsewhere, the character of Friday in Defoe's *Robinson Crusoe* is 'the prototype of the successful colonial subject' (*CPR* 187). But, for Spivak, the 'production' of 'the international neo-colonial subject' is 'different from the production of the *colonial* subject' ('Political Economy' 223).

What, then, has become of the old colonial subject? Spivak's explanation is that, although for transnational capital with its export-processing zones (EPZs) the neo-colonial subject is representative, superseding the colonial subject in some sense, the role played by the older colonial subject is, at least until the age of global financialization, a residual rather than emergent one: 'In the new nations, they had a strong hand in fashioning a new cultural identity. This did not always dovetail with the cultural-political situation in the metropolis. For the indigenous elite did not have an established new informant position' (*CPR* 359). By the time Spivak writes 'French Feminism in an International Frame', however, the situation has changed (see also *CPR* 360). The persona of that essay is clearly implicated in, and fights against, a matrix of information-retrieval about Third World women. Although Spivak's theorizing about the paradigmatic neo-colonial (or postcolonial) subject as female worker in the EPZ had not fully begun then, there is a rhetorical strategy at work already that will endeavour to connect the women in two worlds with each other – or at least to get the woman of the North to comprehend how her position depends upon that of women in the South.

Such a strategy of reading the world, of fostering what Spivak later calls 'transnational literacy' may be compared with the work of German sociologist Maria Mies. Writing at nearly the same time in *Patriarchy and Accumulation on a World Scale: Women in the International Division of Labour*

(1986), Mies powerfully analyses the international division of labour. Mies asks her Northern readers to see that:

> the new IDL divides up the world into producers and consumers, but it also divides women internationally and class-wise into producers and consumers. This relationship is structured in such a way that Third World women are *objectively* – not *subjectively* – linked to First World women *through the commodities* which the latter buy. This is not only a contradictory relationship, but also one in which the two actors on each side of the globe do not know anything of each other. (*Patriarchy* 120–1)

If, for Mies, this analysis is designed to raise an altered self-awareness – 'women in the rich countries have no objective interest in the maintenance of this integrated system of exploitation . . . because it is [Third World women] who are the "image of the future" . . . also for women in the industrialized nations' (*Patriarchy* 143) – for Spivak the call is ethical. Spivak's initial moves in this direction come in brief remarks in 'French Feminism in an International Frame' – for instance, '[a]t the other end of the spectrum [to the home-buying US female academic], it is th[e] ideologico-material repression of the clitoris as the signifier of the sexed subject that operates the specific oppression of women, as the lowest level of the cheap labor that the multi-national corporations employ by remote control in the extraction of absolute surplus-value in the less developed countries' (*IOW* 153). She is closest to Mies's arithmetic of privilege and exploitation when, in a footnote, she declares that 'even such innocent triumphs as the hiring of more tenured women or adding feminist sessions at a Convention might lead, since most U.S. universities have dubious investments, and most Convention hotels use Third World female labor in a most oppressive way, to the increasing proletarianization of the women of the less developed countries' (*IOW* 291n44). Feminist individualism is thus deeply implicated in the inequities of the international division of labour; and by implication, so is the (post)colonial female subject as metropolitan academic migrant (see *CPR* 360).

When 'absolute surplus value' and the international division of labour are at issue, the emphasis is on industrial capitalism. From Spivak's remarks, however, it is clear that the relationship of the Northern female academic to industrial capitalism in the periphery is mediated through finance capital. Spivak emphasizes investment as well as the consumption of goods and services. When finance capital begins to operate by not only exploiting the labour of metropolitan migrants and citizens in the periphery, but through the direct making of loans, then we have entered a different phase. In this phase, the borrower – the capitalist has always imagined wages to be an advance against anticipated profits, and the worker a debtor – does not need to be a factory worker. He or she will regulate his or her own working day in order to extract the absolute surplus value necessary to generate the money to pay back the interest on the loans. It is to Spivak's analysis of the position of the NI in this phase of the system that I now turn.

'Gender and development' and the financialization of the globe

Where is feminism set to work today? Spivak answers this question systematically in a number of recent works. *A Critique of Postcolonial Reason* could only consider 'the civilizing mission of today's universalist feminism' and 'the rôle of the UN-style initiative in the New World Order in the pores of this book' (*CPR* 13n), adding brief but telling discussions of financialization and credit-baiting in footnotes and parentheses (*CPR* 250, 252, 361). The upshot of these remarks, made by 'one woman teetering on the *socle mouvant* of the history of the vanishing present' (*CPR* 359), is that world trade and wage labour have taken a back seat to finance capital, and that feminists advocating micro-loans may be part of a problem rather than a solution (*CPR* 102n, 220n). Spivak's big book stages the impossibility of saying everything, of capturing the moment as it runs away from the writer. It thus gestures towards the elements of the new world order that will, by the time *A Critique* is published in 1999, already have become the principal preoccupation of Spivak's interventions, all over the world, as a theorist of women in global capitalism. Along with her most recent rereading of Marx, they are perhaps the most exciting part of Spivak's oeuvre – displaying a mind attempting to follow, and engage philosophically, developments up to the minute.

Until *Red Thread* appears, it will not be possible to learn the level of synthesis Spivak has reached on these questions. There are, however, formulations in numerous texts, produced for a wide range of different occasions, that show the outlines of a theory. One of the most accessible is Spivak's contribution to the forum on 'American Gender Studies Today' published in *Women: A Cultural Review* in 1999. While, as I have observed, Camille Paglia uses that forum to advocate a benevolent imperialist feminism, Spivak conducts an analysis of the systemic conjuncture, and the agency of feminists within it. Feminist agency has become regularized in 'transnational agencies':

> Gender issues are now in the hands of the transnational agencies and the United Nations. The World Bank changed its 'Women in Development' rubric to 'Gender and Development,' in conjunction, I believe, with the Fourth World Women's Conference in Beijing in 1995. Whatever the theorization about gender might amount to, these efforts have a general, broad colloquial understanding of the word 'woman,' and try to engage in the betterment of the lives of people and groups thus presupposed in terms of poverty, education and training, health, violence, armed conflict, economy, decision-making, institutional mechanisms, human rights, media, environment, the girl-child, and institutional and financial arrangements.

These are the 'areas of concern' of the Platform of Action issued by the Beijing conference. If you notice, economic and activist issues are mixed up there. That mixture indicates the ways in which economic restructuring can take gender issues as its ostensible purpose. By economic restructuring I mean, first, the removal of barriers between national economies and international capital in order that the same system of exchange can be established all over the world and thus reduce the possibility of constitutional redress, and, second, control over central banking systems for the free flow of finance capital.

The move towards the use of gendering in the interest of the global economy started as early as the Declaration of Mexico in 1975. The initial project of making women equal partners in a 'new world economic order' was certainly well intentioned, but impractical in the reality of the global economy and geopolitics. Soon, the pharmaceutical investments in population control and seed/fertilizer control began to affect subaltern women's lives in an adverse way, without the possibility of infrastructural openings for a grassroots critique to make itself heard. By 'subaltern,' I mean persons with little access to social mobility, not all classes of persons of colour in metropolitan space.

'Women in Development' seemed to promise social mobility in the lowest reaches by bringing women into foreign, direct-investment manufacturing – especially textiles and electronics – and export processing zones. The inequities of that situation have been much reported on. 'Gender and Development,' however, seems to give a more equitable opportunity to subaltern women by offering them micro-credit for micro-enterprise. This is, in principle, a good thing but, in fact, often is no more than a way of making a huge untapped market available to the commercial sector. This is because the great wave of such initiatives today do not resemble pioneer organizations such as the Self-Employed Women's Association (SEWA), which started from the establishment of a bank, and was centrally interested only in infrastructural change and working through the women's cultural base into a model of freedom. Today the quick micro-credit initiatives are not interested in infrastructural change, are intrinsically tied to transnational agencies and, what matters most in the field of gender issues, engage in training northern field workers to give what is called 'gender training' to subaltern women in order that they become appropriate receivers and servicers of credit. If there is any field where gender issues should be engaged, it is in the examination of the contrast between the earlier efforts and these contemporary efforts which are now appropriating the earlier ones. ('American Gender Studies' 217–18)

A great deal is packed into these four paragraphs. The most striking thing is that Spivak asserts a relationship between rapidly changing forms of capitalism and the types of international feminist activism conducted on behalf of women in the South. Linked to transnational lending agencies, each of the programmes is implicated in 'development' viewed as increased integration into the world economy. The programme of 'Women in Development', stemming from the Declaration of Mexico of 1975, went hand in hand with the system of wage labour prevalent in EPZs, which Spivak had linked to neo-colonialism in 'The Political Economy of Women'. By contrast, 'Gender and Development' corresponds to the ascendency of finance capital and its direct accessing of the rural women, to whom Spivak refers as 'subaltern'. At a time when the mainstream media in the North uncritically celebrate Grameen Bank, which lends to women in Bangladesh, Spivak places such initiatives in context. They are, first of all, linked to transnational agencies – hence, subaltern rural women are led directly into the global economy, without the protections of the state. Second of all, they do not bring about infrastructural change.

Spivak is particularly critical of 'gender training' – the name given by international agencies to their efforts to raise consciousness about gender inequality.[10] Implicit in Spivak's criticisms is the sense that gender training is an endeavour to foster possessive individualism among women of the South.

Quick-fix free choice for women has been my object of study for twenty years, ever since I started working on Sati. 'Gender trainers,' offering to manufacture 'free choice,' try to center culturally different subjects into decisionmaking without adequately preparing themselves. . . . 'Gender training,' touching subject production with superficial gestures of respect, visits the greatest violation of cultural integrity, in the interest of capital, by means of women upon women. ('Other Things Are Never Equal' 42–3).

Spivak's contribution to the forum on 'American Gender Studies Today' is a schematic description of a conjuncture and confluence of agencies. Spivak addresses the theoretical implications for feminism in a number of other texts. She writes elsewhere that '[i]f the colonial subject was largely a class subject, and if the subject of postcoloniality was variously racialized, then the subject of globalisation is gendered. . . . The target of . . . international civil society is Woman' ('Claiming Transformation' 123; cf. 'Other Things Are Never Equal' 41–2). If this is the case, then agency has shifted – if not entirely away from those 'like' herself: the postcolonial NI – towards the rural subaltern woman: 'a general gendered will for globalisation is being constituted. This is the female client of micro-credit' ('Claiming Transformation' 124).

What is left for the feminist theorist to do? Spivak's answer lies in education; if a teacher of literature can uncoercively rearrange the desires of students at an American university, there must be a way of uncoercively touching the mental theatre of the subaltern woman (see 'Moral Dilemma'), of speaking *to* her, as 'French Feminism in an International Frame' stipulated long before Spivak actively involved herself in rural education. An alternative to 'gender training' is imaginable: 'If one wishes to create an appropriate gender dynamic, whose foregone conclusion is not suitability for capital servicing, a great deal of non-anthropologizing patience is required' ('Other Things Are Never Equal' 43). What she means by this is set out in more detail when she discusses rural teacher training in 'Righting Wrongs' and the other recent texts I discussed in Chapter 1. The invocation, by referring to a 'general will', of Rousseau in *The Social Contract* is a clue that, for Spivak, the uncoercive rearrangement of desire or will is profoundly linked to democracy – and to its manipulation by transnational agencies acting, ultimately, in the interests of global capital. Rural schools are not likely to overturn the system; they are just a permanent parabasis operating otherwise to the main system of meaning ('Other Things Are Never Equal' 42; cf. *CPR* 430).

As a teacher, Spivak is implicated at both ends of the world. Training in literacy in the rural South begins to function as a metaphor for instruction in literary reading in the Northern academy, which must include a development of transnational literacy. Reading the world leads to teaching others to read the world. This is how Spivak has answered, in practice, the questions with which I opened this book: How might responsibility in today's world be understood by the literary reader? Can training in a literary habit of reading give a special character to ethical and political responsibility? Can reading, in any sense of the word, lead to a responsible global literacy? In my final chapter, I examine Spivak's response to two interlinked issues that, from the vantage of a North America in which news and propaganda are at times scarcely distinguishable, have saturated one's sense of the present global conjuncture: war, and suicide as an act of war.

Notes

1 In the Foreword to *Other Asias*, Spivak affiliates her occasional writings with the familiar essay as exemplified by Charles Lamb in *Essays of Elia* (1800), a book she read when it was a set text for the English Honours baccalaureate at Presidency College in the 1950s.

2 As I noted in Chapter 2, in *A Critique of Postcolonial Reason*, Spivak mistakenly gives the date of the Cerisy colloquium as 1982.

3 Responding to a review of *A Critique of Postcolonial Reason* that began by referring to her as 'the great grand-daughter of a land owner', Spivak writes: 'For the record, my father's father, Harish Chandra Chakravorty, was the estate manager of the *zamindar* of Gauripur and never sat down in his presence' ('Reason and Response').

4 Commenting on Irigaray in an interview published in 1993, Spivak makes explicit how she engages French feminist writing in accordance with the stylistic protocols of the avant-garde: 'I like reading Irigaray, but I read her within the general tradition of French experimental writing, foregrounding rhetoric. It is only if she is read as the pure theoretical prose of truth – whatever that might be – that she may seem essentialist when she talks about women' (*OTM* 17).

5 See also 'Burden of English'.

6 Spivak reads J.M. Coetzee's *Foe* (1986) in similar terms: '*He* is involved in a historically implausible but politically provocative revision. He attempts to represent the bourgeois individualist woman in early capitalism as the *agent* of *other*-directed ethics rather than as a combatant in the preferential ethics of self-interest; as the counterfigure to Jane Eyre, as a strictured complication of Kipling's William' (*CPR* 182).

7 As it does also in 'Political Economy of Women' (220).

8 See also 'Setting to Work' (167).

9 Spivak thus straddles the 'idealist' and 'materialist' predications of the subject set out at the beginning of 'Scattered Speculations on the Question of Value': 'The modern "idealist" predication of the subject is consciousness. Labor-power is a "materialist" predication' (*IOW* 154).

10 For more details on gender training, see Cummings, Van Dam and Valk, eds, *Gender Training*.

Chapter 5

Thoughts on War and Suicide

> I started from the conviction that there is no response to war.
> War is a cruel caricature of what in us can respond. You cannot
> be answerable to war.
> Yet one cannot remain silent.
> – 'Terror: A Speech after 9–11'

War

War forces the intellectual to respond. But when force is involved, is
one's answer truly a response? The answer for Spivak is no, not really.
Yet one speaks. Words accumulate in the air and on the page. Forced to
talk, one's words are hopelessly contaminated by the atmosphere of
wartime. No matter how closely one abides by the truth, war is an
occasion for speaking that makes a fool of purity. War makes one take
sides. Its appeal is a recruiting call. See if you can maintain neutrality, it
blares. I dare you to respond in the name of peace, of humanity. I dare
you to tell the truth, and, as I compel from you an answer, I challenge
you to eschew force. Freud found himself in this predicament. The two
parts of his 'Thoughts for the Times on War and Death' (1915), in turn,
acknowledge the pull of partisanship, and strive to elude the currents of
the times by entering into reflection. The double gesture negotiates
the oxymoron of the forced response. 'Thoughts' is added to the title
by the English translator, as if to insist that a certain refutation of
Nietzschean untimeliness is entertained in the more elliptical German
title, 'Zeitgemässes über Krieg und Tod'. But there is, and can be, no
refutation of untimeliness. And it is surely not what Freud sought. Of a
time, thoughts or observations are never quite in time. They aim at
another time – a time of reception when, perhaps, the conflict will have
passed; and, since this is the condition of possibility for writing, a time

when the writer will have died. Such thoughts judge present conflict in the name of that future perfect, just as those thoughts will be judged by a posterity with no stake in it (if there is ever such a posterity).

In the second of his essays, Freud turned to 'Our Attitude towards Death'. The unconscious death-wish is primary; love is a reaction, elaborated across millennia of culture, against this hostile impulse within us, but it is, relatively speaking, a thin accretion, and wars between peoples are inevitable. In his peroration, Freud recommends adaptation. 'If you want to endure life,' Freud writes, rephrasing an old saw, 'prepare yourself for death' (300). Alongside this bit of advice 'in keeping with the times', and mirroring the future perfect, is a picture of a time that once was, when even the enemy was included in the commandment: 'Thou shalt not kill.' 'This final extension of the commandment', Freud observes, 'is no longer experienced by civilized man', who will return from the war that is destroying Europe without a pang of guilt. Elsewhere, though, where they 'still survive in the world . . . [s]avages – Australians, Bushmen, Tierra del Fuegans – are far from being remorseless murderers', atoning for murders when they return from war 'by penances which are often long and tedious' (295). Savages 'act differently' (295). The savages are thus the example for how human beings of culture (*Kultur* is the word translated by 'civilization') can do otherwise than they do, and can even turn against themselves, or a part of themselves, as they turn towards the enemy – not in enmity but in love.

The war to which Spivak responds is 'America's war on terrorism' ('Terror' 81). This 'war', initiated by Ronald Reagan and continued under Bill Clinton, was pursued with intensified zeal after September 11, 2001, when passenger aircraft were hijacked and flown into the Twin Towers of the World Trade Center in New York City and into the Pentagon in Washington, DC by young men linked to Osama bin Laden's Al-Qaeda network, killing themselves and about 3,000 other people. In response, the United States, in alliance with other countries, invaded Afghanistan in December 2001. On the false pretext that Saddam Hussein had developed and intended to mobilize 'weapons of mass destruction', an American-dominated coalition attacked and occupied Iraq in March 2003.

Two questions inform Spivak's 'Terror: A Speech after 9–11' (2004): 'What are some already existing responses? And, how respond in the face of the impossibility of response?' ('Terror' 81). Without making the figure of the Aboriginal her example, as she does in a way uncannily shadowing Freud when alluding to ethical practices 'defective for capitalism', Spivak takes up his endeavour to write of the times without succumbing to them. This effort generates, as in Freud, a productive untimeliness. When Spivak senses the force of war to compel a response that is, properly speaking, not really a *response*, it is to a part of the human apparatus that can be altered, even altered without force, that she turns. Drawing on the ethico-poetic genealogy that I discussed in Chapter 1, she calls that part the imagination. For Spivak, this faculty is linked to desiring, and is activated through reading, which is the medium par excellence for the Humanities 'understood as an uncoercive rearrangement of desires' ('Terror' 81). This idea has been taken up by Spivak in a number of texts in the last ten years. In 'Terror', however, it gathers an immediate urgency – for it is war that militates against it, coercing desires, and forcing a response that is not really a response.

Spivak's response is pointedly different from that of Noam Chomsky. No lasting peace will be achieved, Spivak writes, '[u]nless we are trained into imagining the other' ('Terror' 83). This is distinct from identifying the perpetrators and putting them on trial, something that Chomsky repeatedly advocates in the interviews in *9–11* over going to war against Afghanistan (*9–11* 23–6 and *passim*). For Spivak 'politico-legal calculation' is not an alternative. Training into imagining the other is also 'training . . . into a preparation for the eruption of the ethical'. As Spivak explains, drawing as she has elsewhere from Derrida and Levinas, '[t]he ethical interrupts [epistemological construction and legal calculus] imperfectly, to listen to the other as if it were a self, neither to punish nor to acquit' ('Terror' 83; cf. 95).

It is in this light that Spivak questions Chomsky's notion that ' "globalization," or "economic imperialism," or "cultural values," [are] matters that are utterly unfamiliar to bin Laden and his associates and of no concern to them' ('Terror' 88; see Chomsky, *9–11* 31). This is, in Spivak's eyes, a failure of imagination: 'If, on the other hand, we think of the actants involved, politicized graduate students, rather unlike Chomsky's stereotype, we do not have to withhold from them the bitterness of understanding' that their cities and countries might be bypassed by the benefits of globalization and world trade ('Terror' 88). They, at least, would have some awareness of the 'Great Game' played by the major powers since the nineteenth century for control of central Asia ('Terror' 88; see also 'Foucault and Najibullah', 'Globalicities' 81).

Suicide

As an enemy, the suicide bomber is a special case. Noting that, in the rites of mourning after September 11, the hijackers were unremembered ('Terror' 89–90), a sign that public criticism was reneging on its task of relating to the enemy through the imagination, Spivak proposes an application of her ideas to the suicide bomber. On the one hand, in contrast to the Humanities teaching that she describes as an uncoerced rearranging of desires, in the case of the suicide bomber we have 'coerced yet willed suicidal "terror" . . . groups such as Hamas or Islamic Jihad . . . coercively rearrange desires until coercion seems identical with the will of the coerced' ('Terror' 93). On the other hand, 'we must be able to imagine our opponent as a human being, and to understand the significance of his or her action. It is in this belief – not to endorse suicide bombing but to be on the way to its end, however remote – that I have tried to imagine what message it might contain' ('Terror' 93). What they did may, in the imagination of the hijackers, have been the destruction of a temple ('Terror' 91).

Yet the message may not have so identifiable a content. It may be performative rather than constative. 'Suicidal resistance is a message inscribed in the body when no other means will get through', Spivak writes. 'It is both execution and mourning, for both self and other, where you die with me for the same cause, no matter which side you are on, with the implication that there is no dishonor in such shared death' ('Terror' 96).[1] At every turn, Spivak registers the risk of censure.[2] Her sense of the suicide bomber as 'imaginative actant' ('Terror' 94) is not derived from information gathered through fieldwork. Spivak's construction is speculative, or, better still, imaginative. It is, strictly speaking, unverifiable (cf. 'Terror' 109). What matters is not whether it is right or wrong, and that the message has been misunderstood, but that by attributing imagination and the capacity for symbol-formation (inscribing a message) to the enemy, it opens an ethical relation to him or, increasingly in Palestine, her ('Terror' 96).[3] This is, naturally, not the same as mollifying the 'terrorist' with poetry, which is what happens in a bathetic and parodic plea for Culture in Ian McEwan's *Saturday* (2005).

It is with the effort of deciphering that the ethical relation opens. Just as with the childhood memory about the washerwomen (see Chapter 4), this effort carries forth a vocation. It is, as Spivak reminds us, a task that she first took up more than two decades ago: 'Bhubaneswari Bhaduri, the subaltern in "Can the Subaltern Speak?" was a woman who used her gendered body to inscribe an unheard message' ('Terror' 97).

Bhaduri had been entrusted with a political assassination, and, Spivak believes, rather than carry out a murder, took her own life. In order to preempt anyone interpreting her suicide as the outcome of an illicit love affair (the view taken by her descendants), Spivak imagines, she waited until she was menstruating so that it would be clear that she was not pregnant (*CPR* 306–7). Spivak knows that she might be mistaken in her construction, yet the very fact of undertaking the deciphering that she does, makes it possible for her, insofar as it enables her to be read, to speak – although, as Spivak specifies, it does not give her a *voice* (*Post-Colonial Critic* 57). The alternative to such interceptive decoding is silence, or the foreclosure of applying the sexist script of her female relatives. The parallel in 'Terror' is Chomsky's confident assertion that for the hijackers the effects of globalization were of no concern. When such foreclosure takes place, as Spivak says repeatedly in her essay, the subaltern cannot speak.

'Can the Subaltern Speak?' and other writings from around the same time help to bring to light another dimension to Spivak's reflections on suicide bombing. When Spivak writes, in more than one of her recent essays, of suicide bombing as 'a purposive self-annihilation, a confrontation between oneself and oneself – the extreme end of autoeroticism, killing oneself as other, in the process killing others' ('Terror' 95; also see 'Globalicities' 84, 'Ethics and Politics' 21), her emphasis turns to the meaning of suicide rather than to the meaning of a particular act of suicide that may be implicated in suicide bombing as in 9–11. This does not mean, of course, that particular scripts do not guide such acts. In fact, the analysis of such scripts has always been a large part of Spivak's thinking on suicide.

In 'A Literary Representation of the Subaltern', Spivak reads as suicide the death of Jashoda in Devi's 'Stanadāyini' ('Breast-Giver') from a cancer that she refuses to have treated. As part of her revision of psychoanalysis in the Indian context,[4] Spivak introduces the concept of 'regulative psychobiography' (*IOW* 261). 'Rather than the stories of Oedipus (signification) and Adam (salvation), the multiple narratives of situated suicide might', Spivak proposes, 'regulate a specifically "Hindu" sense of the progress of life' (*IOW* 261). Referring to the final paragraphs of 'Breast-Giver', Spivak asks a series of questions:

> Is it possible that, because Mahasweta Devi does not present this conclusion from a male-gendered position, we are not reduced to man's affective diminution when he puts woman in the place of God? Is it possible that we have here, not the discourse of castration

but of sanctioned suicide? 'Jashoda was God manifest, others do and did whatever she thought. Jashoda's death was also the death of God.' Does Jashoda's death spell out a species of *icchamrityu* – willed death – the most benign form of sanctioned suicide within Hindu regulative psychobiography? Can a woman have access to *icchamrityu* – a category of suicide arising out of *tatvajnana* or the knowledge of the 'it'-ness of the subject? The question of gendering here is not psychoanalytic or counterpsychoanalytic. It is the question of woman's access to that paradox of the knowledge of the limits of knowledge where the strongest assertion of agency, to negate the possibility of agency, cannot be an example of itself as suicide. 'Stanadayini' affirms this access through the (dis)figuring of the Other in the (woman's) body rather than the possibility of transcendence in the (man's) mind. (*IOW* 262; embedded quotation from *IOW* 240)

Devi's story figuratively affirms an access that, generally speaking, is not open to the female suicide. In order to pursue this question, Spivak turns to *sati*, or widow self-immolation. In 'Can the Subaltern Speak?' Spivak specifies that the 'philosophical space [of *icchamrityu* and *tatvajñāna*] does not accommodate the self-immolating woman' (*CPR* 292). The question is, then: how *is sati* suicide justified? This leads Spivak into the complex analysis of Hindu scripture that anticipates her reading of Bhubaneswari Bhaduri's suicide. In short, Spivak interprets *sati* as an extreme case of the constitution of the female subject.[5] This she does against the grain of the orthodox Brahmanic Hindu view that the act of *sati* is exceptional – the way in which the widow, denied access to *samnyāsa*, the life-stage of asceticism open to men, can evade the stasis of *brahmacarya* attendant on the death of her husband.[6] The *sati*, in effect, remains the wife instead of reverting to the stasis prescribed for widows (*CPR* 298–303). Observing that, when *sati* was outlawed in the nineteenth century:

> there was no debate on this nonexceptional fate of widows – either among Hindus or between Hindus and British – than that the *exceptional* prescription of self-immolation was actively contested. . . . This legally programmed asymmetry in the status of the subject, which effectively defines the woman as object of *one* husband, obviously operates in the interest of the legally symmetrical subject-status of the male. The self-immolation of the widow thereby becomes the extreme case of the general law rather than an exception to it. (*CPR* 299)

It is to this 'general law' and the regulative psychobiography that it imposes that Bhubaneswari's suicide refers. 'While waiting [for the onset of menstruation]', Spivak speculates, 'the *brahmacārini* who was no doubt looking forward to good wifehood, perhaps rewrote the social text of *sati*-suicide in an interventionist way' (*CPR* 307). This rewriting is not an overturning, but a manipulation, of the regulative psychobiography in which she is inscribed. She writes her death over against the orthodox trajectory of female life and self-administered death. 'She generalized the sanctioned motive for female suicide', Spivak continues, 'by taking immense trouble to displace (not merely deny), in the physiological inscription of her body, its imprisonment within legitimate passion by a single male. . . . The displacing gesture – waiting for menstruation – is at first a reversal of the interdict against a menstruating widow's right to immolate herself' (*CPR* 307). Bhaduri therefore, Spivak implies, asserts access – despite the stories that her relatives, reading her suicide as '*sati*', pass down that introduce as protagonist the dead man (father) or absent man (husband) (*CPR* 307) – to a willed death that, in terms of the regulative psychobiography, does not accommodate the widow.

Spivak's sense of Bhaduri's motive is simple: 'Unable to confront the [political assassination entrusted to her] and yet aware of the practical need for trust, she killed herself' (*CPR* 307).[7] This is a very powerful account of the meaning that she gave her death. Suicide in order not to commit murder. In the revisions to 'Can the Subaltern Speak?' for *A Critique of Postcolonial Reason* one of the things that stands out is a tacit juxtaposition of her suicide to that of the suicide bomber. The latter fully embraces the regulative psychobiography in which the cause is identified with the husband onto whose funeral pyre the widow places her life. Free will is, as it is for the *sati* (*CPR* 298–300), effaced the moment that it is located:

> As in the case of war, martyrdom, 'terrorism' – self-sacrifice in general – the 'felicitous' *sati* may have (been imagined to have) thought she was exceeding and transcending the ethical. That is its danger. Not all soldiers die unwillingly. And there are female suicide bombers. . . . *Sati* could not . . . be read [by the British] . . . with war, with the husband standing in for the sovereign or the state, for whose sake an intoxicating ideology of self-sacrifice can be mobilized. (*CPR* 296–8)[8]

In Spivak's most recent writings, such ideology is viewed to work through a coercive rearrangement of desires.

Spivak does not enter into the regulative psychobiographies that might inform the female suicide bombers of whom she writes in 'Terror: A Speech after 9–11'. If, however, the enemy is to be regarded as an imaginative actant, the careful tracking will have to be done by others. One might also suspect that among those actants, who take the lives of others as they take their own, there will be one or two who, like Bhubaneswari Bhaduri, would rather take their own life than take that of another.

There is a pathos when Spivak's reading of the world, the attention to the idiom that she commends in transnational literacy, comes down, in the case of suicide and suicide bombing, to a reading of the body. Postmortem decipherings, such analyses are always already too late. Even as they trace the bounds of lives as they were circumscribed by life stories of various stamps imprinted in the psyche to be lived out and died by, they have no power to prevent deaths that, apart from the tales that attach to them, are entirely futile. It is that slight difference, of meaning, that perhaps marks the difference between a taking of sides and a response to war, that, although searching for sense in the enemy's willingness to die, is no approval of that sacrifice.

Notes

1   Later in her essay, Spivak invokes the words of Martin Luther King, Jr. from 'Beyond Vietnam', a speech he delivered in New York in 1967: ' "How do they judge us?" King asked. "When they do not leap to negotiate, these things must be remembered," he said' ('Terror' 99). Although powerful, with the notion of the other as *judge* King's words veer into the eschatological and the apportioning of guilt and just desert. They thereby commit themselves to an alternative that Spivak had rejected: 'It cannot be condoned as a legitimate result of bad US policy abroad, as in the usual US-centered political analyses' ('Terror' 95).

2   'It is only the young whose desires can be so drastically rearranged', Spivak adds. 'I have no sympathy for those who train the young in this way' ('Terror' 96).

3   Spivak enters into the background only schematically: 'It is also true that a millennial confrontation is on record, as soon as Islam emerged out of its tribality, of which I as a Europeanist know the European side rather more. George W. Bush, if he were literate, could tap the *Chanson de Roland*. Was it ever thus? I cannot know. Culture is its own explanations. Sayyid Qutb and Sheikh Ahmed Yassin tap into this too' ('Terror' 88–9).

4   For Spivak on psychoanalysis, see also 'Psychoanalysis in Left Field', 'Claiming Transformation', 'Lives' and 'Echo'.

5   The extended commentary on these pages by Shetty and Bellamy ('Post-colonialism's Archive Fever' 36–44) is indispensable.

6   The general law for widows, that they should observe *brahmacarya*, was, however, hardly ever debated. It is not enough to translate *brahmacarya* as 'celibacy.' It should be recognized that, of the four ages of being in Hindu (or Brahmanical) *regulative* psychobiography, *brahmacarya* is the social practice anterior to the kinship inscription of marriage. The man – widower or husband – graduates though *vānaprastha* (forest life) into the mature celibacy and renunciation of *samnyāsa* (laying aside). The woman as wife is indispensable for *gārhastya*, or householdership, and may accompany her husband into forest life. She has no access (according to Brahmanical sanction) to the final celibacy of asceticism, or *samnyāsa*. The woman as widow, by the general law of sacred doctrine, must regress to an anteriority transformed into stasis. (*CPR* 298)

7   Morton infers from what Spivak says that Bhubaneswari 'committed suicide in order to avoid capture by the British colonial authorities' (*Gayatri Chakravorty Spivak* 33). He succinctly concludes that 'Bhubaneswari . . . attempted to cover up her involvement with the resistance movement through an elaborate suicide ritual that *resembled* the ancient practice of Hindu widow sacrifice' (64), but confuses matters when he writes that 'Bhubaneswari's exceptional act of women's resistance during the independence struggle of the 1920s is disguised as an act of *sati*-suicide' (66) when he means that her resistance was disguised *by* the act. If anything, I am arguing, if Spivak is correct about the uncompleted assassination mission, her suicide was an act of desisting rather than of straightforward resistance.

8   The first four sentences were added in *A Critique of Postcolonial Reason*.

Interview with Gayatri Chakravorty Spivak

Mark Sanders (MS): In writing a book about your work for a series entitled 'Live Theory', what has most occupied me are the changes and developments that have taken place in your thinking over the years. The questions I have for you relate mainly to those changes. Let me open with this one: In the appendix to *A Critique of Postcolonial Reason* you point to an ethical turn in Derrida: the shift in emphasis from 'guarding the question' to the 'call to the wholly other'. You date this to the Cerisy colloquium of 1980 on 'The Ends of Man', where you heard Derrida, his work under intense discussion, make an unrehearsed response to a paper by Jean-Luc Nancy. This, for you, is a key moment in the 'setting to work of deconstruction'. In the last decade or more, you have explicitly taken up the topic of ethics in a number of texts. Did your work take an 'ethical turn' of its own? Was there an identifiable turning point for you? Does your occupation with the ethical predate your *explicit* engagement with ethics?

Gayatri Chakravorty Spivak (GCS): All these answers are of course in terms of my stereotype of myself. They should be considered a text rather than the authoritative account. Given what I am I am deeply suspicious of one's own understanding of one's own trajectory, so I think as long as I am confident that you and your readers will take this as a text I can really let myself go, as my stereotype of myself. I certainly myself felt Derrida's ethical turn at Cerisy, but since then, especially in *Voyous*,[1] Derrida has been very careful to say that in fact the ethical was there right from the start. I think therefore both things are true: that it was there right from the start, and that there was a turn. The two earlier texts that he mentions as being most inclined toward the ethical are the two texts that I also think of. One is 'Différance'[2] and the other is *Of Grammatology*.

MS: And 'Violence and Metaphysics'?

GCS: He doesn't mention that. No. He mentioned those two. And I too think of those. 'Violence and Metaphysics' is *about* ethics. That's a different thing. So I will say that it's both true and not true. It would not have been immediately clear to a reader that the ethical was so strongly present in 'Différance' and *Of Grammatology*. On the other hand, when Derrida actually says it, it is abundantly clear that that is so. As for myself! I began thinking about it when I saw the question. No, it does not correspond to Derrida's ethical turn. When I started teaching Marx in 1978 it was clear right from the start that I was interested in the question of the possibility of a socialist ethics. Because it seemed that ethics was a dirty word for academic Marxists in the United States; one had to keep focused on politics. World-historically this seemed to me to be perhaps a denegation. The possible answers to the problematic of that question have changed over the years for me. But I was interested in this right then. In 1986, my colleague, Joe Camp, in the philosophy department at the University of Pittsburgh, gave me a manuscript by a man called Railton on socialist ethics.

MS: Yes, I remember the manuscript.

GCS: My interest was later enriched by work on what I perceived to be Derrida's ethical turn and then through Derrida on Levinas but it began at least as early as '78. The question: is it possible to have an ethics that would be consonant with the rationalism of socialism? That's how I began.

MS: It's interesting that you date that turn in your own work to 1978, which is a little earlier than I would date it, having looked at your published work. My guess would have been a little later, looking at 'French Feminism in an International Frame', where there is a preoccupation with speaking *to* the other woman. That seemed to me to mark a very important ethical turn, at least in your published work.

GCS: Yes.

MS: Which seemed to anticipate some of the things that Derrida himself would enter into.

GCS: Well, I don't know about anticipation. That's for readers. But I would say that already in . . . Well, as I say, my teacherly interest and my thinking interest is '78. And that particular interest then expressed itself in terms of women already in 'Can the Subaltern Speak?', a paper that was given in 1982. There the question was: is a woman's ethics located between her legs and fixated upon a unique male? Simple questions, important ones. Now, interestingly, you find it in 'French Feminism in an International Frame', whereas, in my sense of my own itinerary, it is 'Can the Subaltern Speak?' that stands out. But you're right, of course.

MS: When I reread 'Can the Subaltern Speak?' – and that's one of my next questions – about 'regulative psychobiography' – it seemed to me that readers of that essay miss the fact that you're talking about regulative psychobiography in *life* as well as in death, in suicide. And that that involves the attachment to the single male figure – whether it is the husband or nation or cause. It wasn't something that I had quite grasped when I read it in the past.

GCS: Yes. And no. The story of Oedipus according to Freud is the regulative psychobiography of the human individual. Melanie Klein undid that one. She said that regulative psychobiographies are taken from permissible narratives. Now, I was not working on Melanie Klein then, but why I became so fascinated by Melanie Klein was because that's what I was seeing in the narrative of *sati*. That the Hindu scriptures were providing a regulative psychobiography. People have brought up silly objections to this by saying that, you know, I was bringing in all this Brahminical claptrap to describe very common women, but that is indeed the whole point, that the permissible narratives come from mythic or religious texts ideologically informing society at all levels. In fact I have encountered this in my activism, among subaltern women and women of all races and classes, this idea of how one's life should be lived, according to a story that is already there. . . . The suicide in *sati* is not a suicide. That's the problem. If it could be a suicide, then it would be a very peculiar declaration of an autonomy of will, declared in the quenching of it. Suicide is not a 'sin' in Hinduism. There is a discussion of varieties of suicide in the essay.

MS: So, *sati* is really, from what you write, a version of marriage.

GCS: A displacement of the same theme. So that the death of the woman is just a moment in the story, not important enough to qualify as suicide, whereas the good suicide is willed death.

MS: When did you see a relationship between ethics and literature?

GCS: I'm not very clear on this because my stereotype of myself has just confronted this one. Old hardcore US leftists have been on my case recently for having confidence in literature. I had somehow forgotten that of course when, for example, I wrote that piece on *The Prelude* in the early eighties, I adhered to a version of how to think of literature in the superstructure as it were – a very orthodox kind of Little-Britain Marxism in its US version – I am not sure when. Because for me it was a practical thing. Somewhere along the line, practically, that whole problem of socialist ethics began to resolve itself as the training available in teaching students not to always see their own reflection in literature, or to assert their own diagnostic abilities. It's as simple as that.

MS: So, by 'practically', you mean in teaching?

GCS: I don't know. All kinds of things. But teaching is certainly one of them. I haven't yet constructed a stereotype of this – when it shifted. But Marx had something to do with it, because the *Eighteenth Brumaire*, for me, became an exemplary text. It has to be read for its literariness. For the commanding metaphor of drama – which is a real *concept*-metaphor – and its real importance throughout the text in terms of an understanding of politics in action. It's not just a figurative illustration of an argument. And, secondly, Marx's own use of the logic of rhetoric – the most extraordinary one being that paragraph on proletarian revolution ending in the misquotation of Hegel. And I think that piece, a descriptive piece, which really does not promise anything, unlike the incredible promises of *Capital*, had some role to play somewhere. As early as 'Can the Subaltern Speak?' that passage about representation was deeply influencing me. So, Mark, I cannot give a specific punctual answer to that question: when did it happen? But it did happen. It did happen. I think also reading *Shibboleth*, but that's much later – where Derrida talks about the figure as the experience of the impossible. The teaching of reading, the practice of reading – and this will lead straight into your question about translation – as the preparation for an ethical call that may or may not happen. And also as itself an accountability to a call – the text calls. But I can't say quite when. I know that it happened.

MS: I'm recalling the mid- to late 1990s when you were teaching the history of literary criticism at Columbia. You were following a trajectory of literature and ethics beginning with the Romantics, with Shelley, Wordsworth, I don't remember if Keats was in the mix (but when you refer to 'soul-making' that's Keats, isn't it?). It seems that those figures were there for you at least in the 1990s. Were they there for you before in terms of thinking ethics?

GCS: Not in this way. But yes, sorry, in '78, that year, I was teaching at Texas. And I was teaching 'A Defence of Poetry'. And it was that paragraph, you know, about knowledge explosion and labour-saving devices, and we want the creative faculty to imagine what we know. I can date it because Forest Pyle was in my class. And that became his overriding idea and then he wrote a dissertation on it and then a book on it.[3] You know, the strong imagination. Yes, but, Mark, how can you say it was only the Romantics? You were in my class when I was teaching Plotinus.

MS: I didn't say it was *only* the Romantics . . . When were you reading Plotinus?

GCS: I began a dissertation on Shelley in 1963 and after writing a chapter I let it go. So Plotinus. And then for Yeats the neo-Platonists were incredibly important. I didn't quite make the connection between ethics and literature, but by the time I'm teaching history of lit crit Plotinus is big. Aristotle: the idea of pity and fear being the positive and the negative feeling toward the other. Aristotle as *metis*, you remember, as the Stagirite, not an Athenian citizen. Plato as the *polites*, and so therefore the entire theory structured on the tragic hero as other. Social therapy. Aristotle is quite different, a 'real' philosopher, altogether systematic, when he is actually writing *on* ethics. That's not what I'm talking about. I'm talking about the looser thing in the *Poetics* . . .

MS: Better than philosophy . . . ?

GCS: Better than history.

MS: I have become increasingly interested in your practice as a translator. And how it might have influenced your theories about translation. Emily Apter, for instance, writes in a forthcoming piece about how your texts on translation from the preface to *Of Grammatology*, 'The Politics of Translation', the prefaces and postfaces to your translations of Mahasweta Devi, to the Kleinian thematics of 'Translation as Culture', practically constitute an unwritten book on translation. Have your theories on translation changed? Have you a different sense of the ethics of translation to when you began to translate? I am struck, for instance, by the audacity of your translation of Devi's novel, *Chotti Munda and His*

Arrow – your rendering of Devi's representation of the Bengali of tribals in an idiosyncratic English in a way that appears to relax the stricture adopted by you in your prefatory essay to your translation of Devi's 'Draupadi' in 1981: 'I have had the usual "translator's problems" only with the peculiar Bengali spoken by the tribals. In general we educated Bengalis have the same racist attitude toward it as the late Peter Sellers had toward our English. It would have been embarrassing to have used some version of the language of D.H. Lawrence's "common people" or Faulkner's blacks. Again, the specificity is micrological. I have used "straight English," whatever that may be' (*IOW* 186). What encouraged you to depart so radically from 'straight English' in *Chotti Munda*? Is there any relationship between your evolving translator's practice and your theories about translation, especially in your recent writings on the subject?

GCS: I'd done a lot of translation in between. You know, in 1981, it wasn't just that I thought it was not a good idea, but also I would not have been *able to do it*. I did not have the courage to do it – 'audacity' is a good word. But in 1981 I was also not as turned off as I have been by the great African writers – writers as great as Ngũgĩ in *Petals of Blood* – deciding to express the subjectivity of the subaltern African by a sort of poetic language. I have more sympathy with, let's say, a *Palm-Wine Drinkard*, but that's a different thing. Here I'm making a translation, making up something, so I didn't know how well it would fly. But I must show a debt of gratitude to Andrew McNeilly, my editor at Blackwell, because there was one thing, I now forget what the detail was, I must ask Andrew, look at the correspondence, he said Gayatri you mustn't do this, this is going to make it look funny to most British readers, and so there was one detail that I lifted, I forget what it was. I think it may have been t-apostrophe for 'the'.

MS: With that practice as a translator, what about the theory?

GCS: Well, let me first say something that I have not said in my stuff, although I don't see how any practical translator can not know it. But it's always pleasant when some other person theoretically presents something which you immediately recognize as just astute. You know, Naoki Sakai at Cornell, he at a certain point talked about the effacement of the subjectivity of the translator. It is so correct. But I have never written that. I had written about accessing the other, but it is true that when you translate, very practically, what you want to do is bring out Mahasweta or bring out Derrida. And it would be a fault if the reader felt your presence. So it's practical. And I think that's where one should really start. I think that there is never a place where there is no translation, and this is again why I find Melanie Klein so unbelievable, and, again, you know, Mark, if there is one thing about me which I believe has been influenced by my teachers – and Derrida was never my teacher, but influenced me in such a way that he might as well have been my teacher – I'm a tenacious literalist, and so the fact that Melanie Klein says something so obviously clear that, with these part objects, the child begins to construct an ethical semiosis – now that is an act of, what else would you call it, it's an act of translation. It's a translation that is underived – this is why 'Différance' is so interesting – it is the translation that is the ego (Melanie Klein, after all, is talking about the putting-together of the ego), what the ego must differ from in order to be ego, is that which is being translated. So the original – a bunch of part objects? – is always differed in the space of différance. That is where translation, for me, very practically, begins.

MS: Ethical semiosis is an interesting term, but, I think, quite a complex one. There are two components, 'semiosis' and 'ethical'. How do you see them articulating in originary translation?

GCS: OK. I'm going to give an answer that is slightly crooked. The uncoordinated body (part objects) providing ingredients for ethical semiosis is where the binary opposition between suicide and access to the self – the destruction of the self through willing – becomes undone. That is why I am interested in, as it were, real suicides. In fact there *is* no such thing as suicide, obviously. But . . . Now, what was your question again?

MS: Ethical semiosis . . . why 'semiosis' and why 'ethical?'

GCS: Because, in Melanie Klein's understanding at least – this is a different idea of ethics, isn't it? – when you read, when you love, when you make reparation, which is always in excess of need, all of that comes by the fact that the human child distinguishes between need and desire, pleasure and fulfilment, and that excess is what gives the possibility of saying good and bad. So that is a semiois. On the other hand, strictly speaking, it is just as the call of the other or the gift is not accessible, when it is understood it is understood as responsibility or accountability. Therefore in Derrida it's always 'the gift if there is any' – this is where Derrida is distinguished from Levinas and all of them from Kant. Kant has transcendental deduction, and Levinas has signification. Derrida puts the trace there. Ethical semiosis is responsibility, accountability, etc. And the call of the other is that underived fiction of the original as différance. You understand? So that's what it is. I've never quite said it this way, but I've thought it.

MS: So there are parallels for you between Klein and Derrida?

GCS: I don't know if there are parallels, or if it is me reading actively. Although I will say that both Deleuze and Guattari and Lacan have not been able to acknowledge Klein fully. They have always patronized her as having fallen back into the Oedipal – whereas Klein fell back into the Oedipal as, strictly speaking, a permissible narrative. And also, this idea of the translation and the underived fiction of the original which is always differed, this I was going to put together in a piece on the graphic of the gift, but that never came to be. It gives me pleasure to say it at last.

MS: That's really quite fascinating. What struck me teaching Klein last fall was the derivative status of the father in Klein's story.

GCS: It's wonderful.

MS: If you have Oedipus, it is certainly no point of origin for it. It's completely derivative.

GCS: It displaces itself in the place of the original in what is later called translation – linguistic translation. In order to – the original is not a fixed place – in order to access that original you have to enter into the mysterious thickets of the so-called original language, which is not bound by the text that you are translating, nor is it bound by anything, you know, and because people don't realize this they have the audacity to translate simply because they are so-called native speakers born into the language. That's why we have so much bad translation.

MS: It really struck me, reading many of the things you have written on translation – 'The Politics of Translation' and also 'Translating into English' – that you really stress literary history, and, in 'Translating into English', the presuppositions of the writer – your examples are Kant, Marx and Lacan – these things, on the one hand, seem to be fairly traditional criteria for translation, but from what you were saying a few minutes ago, there are far more profound implications to thinking about the language of the original.

GCS: The original is unlimited. And so, the responsibility of translation is the only way we can understand the limitlessness of the original. Language does not have an outline. At the same time that there are these native-speaker translators who are an abomination, there is also a need to acknowledge that the translator's job is not a hack's job. The old-fashioned translators who are really good, who are not these new-fangled folks who take advantage of the fact that nobody here knows their native language, it has to be acknowledged for their sake that translation is a labour of love. How few of the people who live in the theoretical universe and actually write about translation, how few of them actually do translations!

MS: One so often forgets that, say, 'The Task of the Translator' is Benjamin's preface to his translation of Baudelaire.

GCS: Yes, yes.

MS: And many of your texts on translation are prefaces to your own translations – to Derrida, to Devi . . .

GCS: . . . to Mazhar. Yes. And, you know, there is also that translation of the eighteenth-century hymns which came out only in India.

MS: Song for Kali . . .

GCS: Again, talking about entering into thickets of limitlessness. I ended that book by saying it would be good if I could have these translations looked at by William Merwin because he did such wonderful translations of the *Gītā* without having known Sanskrit. I took them to William Merwin – I love William Merwin, I have nothing against him – but nothing much came out of it. And I think . . . I realized it is because these hymns, which are a kind of tradition which is doubled on the tradition of *bhakti* – doubled on because they are more of a citation of the *bhakti* tradition than pure *bhakti* songs. They of course do not have the same status as Sanskrit which is a solid classical language. So it was a mistake to think that an original is just an original. It's also got its own historical differences. So nothing much happened. I had the pleasure of seeing Merwin's tropical forest and also taking a shower outside . . . you know . . . hidden in trees . . . it was a delight to see him again.

MS: Where was this?

GCS: Maui. The island of Maui. So that one is almost a practical acknowledgement of the limitlessness of the original. Who knew when I started translating the *Grammatology* simply as an act of innocent recklessness that I would be forever on this track?

MS: That's what so intrigues me. Forgive me for saying this, but when I read your book on Yeats, if I had had to guess who the author was, I would never have been able to. Something happened.

GCS: That book is not my dissertation. It was written for young adults. A person at Iowa discouraged me from publishing my dissertation, and I'm not going to name him, but I was a fool, I had no idea that I should be asking my dissertation director rather than the Yeats expert at my place of work. And it is clear that he was troubled by what I had to say in the dissertation. And so, what did I know? I really lived in a world where there was no sense of how to advance a career. I didn't publish it.

MS: So, that part of your dissertation, was that written after you read *Of Grammatology*?

GCS: No. But . . . the fourth chapter tells you why it was that I liked Derrida. If I had the time one of these days I want to revise it and publish it, I think it still can be published. No . . . the Yeats book, I wrote it because I had a friend who was working for Crowell and wanted an author, and it was fun writing it.

MS: I have been fascinated by the trajectory of your writings on Marx. Among other things, by your insistence on Marx's project in *Capital*: to have his implied reader, the industrial worker, see himself not as the victim of capitalism but as the agent of production. In *A Critique of Postcolonial Reason*, you draw an analogy between the implied reader of *Capital* and the implied reader of your book: the NI as metropolitan New Immigrant/Native Informant. The latter is your agent in the Northern metropole in an age when industrial capital is giving way, in terms of relative significance, to finance capital. The NI facilitates what you call the 'credit-baiting' of the poorest women of the rural South, thus generating a 'general will for globalization'. This NI has his or her counterpart in the country of origin. Who, though, is your subaltern agent of finance capital in the South? And what self-understanding of his or her agency might you envision for him or her? In 'From Haverstock Hill to U.S. Classroom, What's Left of Theory?' you write about irony as permanent parabasis, and in 'Righting Wrongs' about ethical systems 'defective for capitalism'. Do these formulations add up to a characterization of agency in the South vis-à-vis finance capital and its possible turning of capitalism towards redistribution? If they do, would you elaborate? What role does rural teacher training have in this arena?

GCS: Not only is the worker not the victim of capitalism but the agent of production but, as such, he or she should be able to study capital rationally and see that the commodification of labour power is a *pharmakon* – it is poison in the hands of capitalism but it can be medicine if regulated by socialism. So, that's Marx's project – homeopathic project – for the worker. So, from this I have never shifted, that I understand this to be Marx's project for the worker. There is much more of course, but this is the core of it. And then the whole idea that the commodification of labour power is reification or fetishism or alienation, etc., these things are to me meaningless. Marx is too counter-intuitive for extremely smart people. My real question, as I said to you before, is: can we be sure that the use of this homeopathy is going to lead to socialism as the habit of redistribution? This is where the question of ethics comes in. And, now you say that I draw an analogy. . . .

MS: My real question was in, let's say, an age of finance capital, in an age of financialization of the globe, how does this translate? Where is the agency located? And what happens with Marx's project when the agent is no longer the factory worker? Is there a different understanding for a different agent?

GCS: The factory worker does not remain a factory worker in the narrative that Marx could not, after all, complete (because *Capital*s two and three are put together by Engels). The factory worker becomes the socialist. In order for the commodification of labour-power to become a weapon – this is in the truly great chapter in *Capital* three on the tendency of the rate of profit to fall – the tendency has to be made into a crisis. Everybody knows that Marx did not articulate the revolutionary subject well enough. But this is the biggest disarticulation: between the worker and the socialist. Since the state is not thought through in Marx. So, today less than ever does one have the right to expect the worker to be the socialist. I think this is why I say again and again that, especially in the global South, the state has to be reinvented. Conservatives in the US want people to think that when the state performs its function it is being a *controlling* state. The state is an instrument and a structure. It's not the nation. So that one can – this is a complicated subject – one can practice critical regionalism and think of something like a transnational state structure which would be different from the imposition of the United Nations or international law, a much bigger framework in the hands of the Security Council, managed by the Group of 8. Finance capital is not subject to the same laws as industrial capital. It's world trade which manages the crisis of finance capital. Finance capital cannot operate by itself. It has to be interrupted by world trade. It is in that space of interruption, in a state structure not only reinvented but persistently kept clean of tendencies toward nationalism and fascism. The factory floor has today been pulverized. So we have to think of the worker as a historically interesting role, which remains interesting wherever there is manufacturing. He or she has not disappeared. Because of the disarticulation between worker and socialist there never was much hope for the dictatorship of the proletariat, quickly taken over by the unreconstructed feudality of the vanguard. And today, there is another disarticulation, between the main theatre of capital, finance – and the hopelessly fragmented working class, riven by nationalism and racism, as the disputes over outsourcing clearly show. As a supplement in the strongest sense to the functioning of this reinvented state in a world economy where the state does not have any redistributive capacities, one looks at the disruptive politics of – the phrase 'social movement' is hard to use now – the disruptive politics that would again and again turn capitalist globalization into redistribution. One might call it socialist globalization rather than capitalist globalization. This is the project for the future.

MS: What I wanted to ask you about, what I'm finding so intriguing about your recent writings on Marx – firstly, there seems to be a hint, in what you're saying about the credit-baiting of rural women in the South, that there is an agent or potential agent, and the question would be: if we draw an analogy with the factory worker, and his or her rational study of capital, what sort of analysis will this agent undertake?

GCS: I don't think that this agent is ready to undertake analysis. My feeling is that Marx could take for granted – and he was not correct because the German social democrats voted in war credits in 1914 – he did not, although his third thesis on Feuerbach did ask presciently 'Who will educate the educators?' – he forgot this when he tried to educate the workers *only* in agency and rationalism. I do believe now, and this is where my work has been, that in order to prepare for this kind of agency, you have to undertake, first of all, the kinds of agricultural work, weaver's work, etc., that Farhad Mazhar is undertaking, but you also have to undertake the kind of work which would see telecommunication (now I'm talking class-differentiated) as instrument of socialization rather than as capitalization. But, among the much larger populace of rural women being credit-baited, etc., what you want to do is prepare for the rearrangement of desires, and prepare to learn from these beings, oppressed in one way or another for centuries, what their desires are – you can never know people's desires – but in terms of working for agency in the classroom there has to be some kind of working hypothesis by which you know the students' desires. Without this kind of painstaking training of not wanting certain kinds of things you will never achieve . . . and this is incredibly inconvenient but there is no other way. It is as inconvenient as exercise rather than taking steroids. It is incredibly inconvenient. Even more inconvenient. I'm looking at this Africa stuff – the Group of 8, George Bush and Tony Blair, and thinking: these people don't know the first thing about how to engage with folks that they have themselves destroyed and are still destroying. And of course they are in bad faith. The rock concerts and African music concerts are all about the politics of convenience-generosity. You do not write a book where you show the rational skeleton of all this oppression and say: OK, boys and girls, you know the rationale now, go forth and build a new world. That was Marx's mistake.

MS: Can you connect this to what you say about activating ethical formations defective for capitalism. Is there some link here? You talk about this in 'Righting Wrongs'.

GCS: It's harder than I thought. When one is directing dissertations one is directing one-on-one, this is never taken to be too small an undertaking, or when one is teaching a seminar one is teaching deliberately only twelve people. This is not thought to be too small an undertaking. We have such double standards, and I myself apologize – I'll say it's very small what I'm doing. It ain't small – it's what I can do. But I'm beginning to find – you see, I learn from my mistakes – that when you try to bring about the rituals and habits of democratic behavior – small 'd' – there is a casualty. Those rituals and habits, the intuitions of access to the public sphere – we are talking about the reasonability of the structures of the state and the structures of democracy – those other ways of being, the disenfranchised ways which were defective for capitalism, have also to be reinvented – and this is the difficult thing to think through – as the performative is transformed into performance. The defective-for-capitalism mindset is the performative mechanism of the disenfranchised group before its access to intuitions of the public sphere, before its access to the habits and rituals rather than merely the arithmetical fact of voting. Before. But as these other pharmakons are used in the teaching for these reasonable structures to become accessible to the children that performative is slowly transformed, one hopes, at a later date, into performance. If it is done at the same time it becomes unexamined cultural indentitarianism, voting blocs, ethnic voting blocs, ethnic conflict. It has to be always *nachträglich*. The performance comes through museumization, the performance comes through curricularization, especially literary and artistic curricularization. Not in the name of cultural identity.

MS: So you're talking about anything but the instrumentalization of culture.

GCS: Yes. So you see that my position now is more nuanced, more informed. In that area I learn from my mistakes . . . What else?

MS: There were some other components to my question on Marx . . .

GCS: There is *no* subaltern agent of finance capital. It is not possible for finance capital to have a subaltern agent. When the subaltern is exploited through credit-baiting, it's a small area of finance capital. The real stuff is data.

MS: You're talking about biopiracy?

GCS: All of that stuff. Biopiracy, patenting of all kinds, DNA patenting, pharmaceutical dumping, you name it. Everything is data. Indigenous knowledge, for sure, intellectual property, yes, but also . . . *everything*. The reason why we cannot have that older agency model is because, if in Marx what animated the value form was the general equivalent, namely money – there was credit and so on – therefore it became dysfunctional as the substance gold and so on, today it is data and so the substance of data has become dysfunctional as learning or knowledge. We cannot have a model whereby the *knowing* agent can save us from the world system as such, working finance capital through telecommunication. Telecommunication, like the gold in the money form, is instrumental to financial equivalence. The knowing agent will *use* the telecommunication form and the data form and will perhaps transform it into something to learn in order to manipulate it for socialist rather than capitalist productivity.

MS: Into knowledge?

GCS: Something upstream from knowledge. Learning and knowledge are already different. Learning, knowledge, information, data. Data is not even information. It's that intuition of Marx, incredibly counter-intuitive but incredibly correct – that that which carries the general equivalent does not function as such. Data cannot function as knowledge or learning. So therefore there is no subaltern agent of finance capital (and the worker was never a subaltern). All you have is this kind of *faith* idea that it can happen – that they used faxes at the time of Tiananmen Square or that you can bring unmediated cyber-literacy to African boys. Those won't work. This is a complicated argument, Mark, but I hope you will see that it is also a practical argument. You can't use data as pharmakon as you could commodified labour power. That's why the model now is disruptive, turning-around, rather than using the thing itself as medicine.

MS: Disruption at the level of data – what would that be?

GCS: It's what – you remember I quote Babu Mathew in 'Megacity' – strategy-driven rather than crisis-driven globalization.[4] So, you use globalized capital for a broader and broader model of the welfare state, something that would *resemble* international socialism, but you cannot *have* international socialism because of that and say: look at what we have. It can only be second hand, it can only be fragmentary, contested, but that's the model. That's why I say it's disruptive. Because the more you go toward globalization – real globalization as a model – the more it's going to move toward capitalism. It's because of that, because the redistributive impulse still works on the subject-agent model of epistemic temporality whereas with data we are not in that temporality and the role of data as pharmakon is limited; even as the role of commodified labour-power as rational pharmakon proved to be limited. People like Castells don't figure this out, so they say that place *has changed* to space, that the given world *has changed* into network society.[5] What they don't realize is that the model of resistance will for ever remain confined to the lineaments of the ethical subject and the understanding of agency, whereas the model of that which is resisted has become unmoored from the subject, which is to be instrumental for knowledge and learning. And we have to deal with this disarticulation – remembering that for Marxism too it was a species of disarticulation that was the problem. The *immanent* logic of capital will produce such disarticulations. That is why we go now toward a disruptive model, a permanent parabasis – when we think of a just world.

MS: You have written a great deal about teaching: teaching literature, teaching rural teachers of literacy in India, Bangladesh, Algeria and now China. Teaching seems to be in your bones. When did you *begin* teaching? Has there ever been a time when you have not viewed yourself as a teacher? How has your awareness of yourself as a teacher influenced your thinking about ethics, reading and literature? The teacher–student relationship seems, for you, to be almost exemplary for ethics.

GCS: Once again, though, I would say, as far as I can tell, the experience of teaching is more like that responsibility-accountability rather than the full-fledged ethical. Because one can't *plan* to be ethical. You know, it's like Aristotle, on the first page of the *Poetics*, there is this play going on between *mimesis* and *poiesis*, *mimesis* and *poiesis*, and Aristotle says: All you can really do is to be as scrupulous in your *mimesis* as possible, and, by *tuche*, *poiesis* might emerge. Now, that's a beautiful model of what we are talking about. You don't think 'I'm being ethical' when you are teaching. What you are really thinking about is: How can I get through?

MS: Exactly.

GCS: How can I get through? Only by knowing what to move. You know what I mean? Just completely intent on that, yes? And the thing is that such effort invariably becomes very closely allied to coercion. Coercion. Even explanation is very closely related to coercion. Making desires move. The uncoercive part of it happens without your intervention – it's like the *poiesis* coming by *tuche*. It surprises you, it is unexpected, you cannot plan the lack of coercion. Americans seem to believe that there is such a thing as deliberate non-hierarchical behaviour. That is a piece of nonsense. The idea is to remove hierarchy rather than deliberately behave as if there is no hierarchy. That is solid bad faith. There will never be a total absence of hierarchy. And that is what's fun in the classroom, it's not that you're being ethical, it's that the ethical might flower.

MS: It might happen. I'm so glad that you made that distinction – between coerced and uncoerced – that the uncoerced is unanticipatable.

GCS: Absolutely, absolutely. You wait upon it. It's not possible to teach without a degree of violence and coercion, however disguised.

MS: Because you have a teacher and a student.

GCS: Absolutely. It's not possible. You asked me when I began teaching. I used to drag people even as a child, people who were quite unwilling to learn, and I was completely unable to teach, but somehow I couldn't imagine that anybody could not know how to read and write. This was such a joke! So, I've always done that. And of course, by the time I was about eleven – I was precocious, as of course you know, I graduated high school at thirteen so I was already in high school – that was when my mother involved me in grading papers – because she worked to make destitute widows employable.

MS: I didn't know that.

GCS: Oh, yes. My mother was the complete model of incredible commitment and activism. In '47 when the partition took place, one never saw Mother because before dawn she was in the railway stations with refugee rehabilitation. But, anyway, she involved me in teaching. One thing you have in India is numbers. So there would be huge numbers of papers to grade. So she really taught me how to grade, how to mark, and, finally, how to fake a signature. Learning to teach by faking the maternal signature, with her collusion, the thematics are extremely rich there, right? So, that was at eleven. Then I began teaching for money at seventeen – when I was coaching English. I have been teaching a long time.

MS: Will your forthcoming books, *Red Thread* and *Other Asias*, reorient your work in significant ways? If so, how?

GCS: Other Asias, yes. *Red Thread*, it's more a drawing out of earlier work, it's more a consideration of how this kind of writing turns one into a permanent persuader – that's the line in *Red Thread*. It's a big book, but that's the line. But in *Other Asias* I'm really trying to cope with the idea of critical regionalism that I was talking about, the idea of named space. Asia as a named space. What do we do with this? Especially since Asia is rising, supposedly. What is it that is rising?

MS: The plural *Asias* seems to suggest that there are *many*.

GCS: That is an argument, that one must not think Asia as simply where one lives or where one is from, or Asia as that abstract data circuit, great network, which stands over against Euro–US, over against Latin America, over against Africa, the huge names of regional networks. Now, I want to think outside the both. You see, I've never willingly wooed cultural identity. In this book there is a little bit of that – because I want to be interpellated as an impossible thing – which is an Asian – it's impossible, if you think about . . .

MS: Can you explain why it's impossible?

GCS: Well, think about west Asia, think about central Asia, I'm not even going into detail, think about south Asia, which is where *we* are, and then think about what Asia-Pacific jumps over – which is the Pacific: Oceania. So, where the hell are you going to get an Asian identity in any real way? There isn't lines of similar languages that can be – you know, a thousand languages that can be interlearnt? No – I mean, learning Chinese is killing me, and if you are going to look at the languages of Tajikistan, Uzbekistan, Turkmenistan, Kirghizstan, all of those places where Russian took hold, the Cyrillic alphabet took hold, how are you going to think through something like an *Asian* multiculturalism? And, there is Turkey entering the European Union – Turkey, which was the first place *called* Asia. So, it's a game: Asia. People who are thinking the post-Soviet postcolonially are thinking Eurasia. So, is Eurasia a place? Asia – the entire thing, something of it you can find in the distinction between the Mediterranean and North Africa and the rest of Africa, but it's not as peculiar as the divisions within Asia. That's why it's an impossible interpellation. It's either plural, and you have to live with that plural interpellation, or it's globalized and the name means nothing, except sectorially, or it's completely narcissistic, which means your own background. So, I hope it will reorient my work a little.

MS: 'Reorient' is a funny word to use.

GCS: Yes. At the moment Armenia is giving me a lot of trouble. Because I am thinking Armenia.

MS: Soviet Armenia?

GCS: Well, you tell me. Soviet, Turkish Armenian, Azerbaijani Armenia, Nagorno Karabakh. Little place. And I just wasn't going to give up. I did not give that piece to *Armenian Review* although they wanted it for their first issue – and I think wisely so. The whole book is all finished, but I worried at Armenia, and I believe that I now have some sense of how to redo that chapter. Once Armenia is done, the book is out. You see the problem? The last sentence of the book is: Now for the rest of the world. Because I really cannot bear to think that one should agitate for one's own cultural identity.

MS: As recently as 2003, you said, in an interview in Honolulu, that you would never write your memoirs. Yet you published a fragment of a memoir in the 2005 special issue of *Critical Inquiry* commemorating Edward Said. What made you change your mind? What will the scope be of your memoir? Will it explore the link between your life and your theory?

GCS: You know what happened. Mark, it's a tragic thing. My mother died. You see, I left Hawai'i and I went to California, and my Mum died that first week. And there was the loss of an archive. I began to feel completely different about writing down my story. I still wasn't thinking about it, but then Tariq Ali told me that Edward had told him that I should, that he should ask me – that also – then I talked to my niece (my sister's daughter): Look, I don't feel like writing memoirs, but Nani, Grandmother, is dead, and there is an archive gone, what do you think? And very seriously, she and I talked, and thought, and she suggested something, and I asked Tariq if the first three chapters could be about the past rather than about me. And he said OK. On the other hand I really don't like the idea of writing memoirs, so I've written very little. I've written one about the foremothers, which I've given for the Columbia conference in honour of Carolyn Heilbrun, at Hopkins and at Rutgers. The Edward chapter is slightly different – because it's about me and my intellectual life. If you saw the one about my foremothers – my great grandmother and my two grandmothers, the woman in 'Can the Subaltern Speak?' who, as you know, was my grandmother's sister – you would see that my interest is really much more in the past than in details of my own life again and again. The funny thing is, when I gave it at Hopkins, and then also this man called Ramachandra Guha who has reviewed the Edward Said issue of *Critical Inquiry*, they say to me: You know, you're talking too much about yourself. And I say, look, this is a memoir – what is one supposed to be talking about in a memoir, do you think?

MS: The fragment in the Edward Said issue seemed to be talking about the life and the theory. This is, of course, the Live Theory interview. Is your memoir going to try to approach that impossible question – of the relationship between the Life and the Theory?

GCS: No. One hopes that it will 'inhabit that impossible crux' – rather than consider the question. And there's a funny story here. I do not have an agent for my academic writings. I am very puritanical. I do not want my reputation to rest on the fact that someone else's living depends upon my having one. On the other hand, the moment I agreed to do this totally uncharacteristic thing – which is writing my memoirs – I got an agent. Now, my agent has told me a number of times that I must not be theoretical and I must only really write my life story. This is not possible for me. So I asked, I complained to my very illustrious friend, who certainly sells a lot of books – Toni Morrison – I said: Toni, what to do? I cannot, it's not interesting for me. How the hell am I not going to be theoretical? So, Toni Morrison in her infinite kindness said a very nice thing – and I may use this sentence with my agent, and I say this with total vanity, since my friend flattered me, why can I not quote it in the spirit of vanity? What Ms. Morrison said was: Gayatri, you're not writing memoirs, you're writing Gayatri Spivak's memoirs! So, you should tell your agent that there has to be theory in it. My last words on the matter, for now.

The interview took place at Ajanta restaurant in Morningside Heights, Manhattan, on 8 July 2005.

Notes

1   Derrida, *Voyous: Deux essais sur la raison* (2003), translated as *Rogues: Two Essays on Reason*.

2   In *Margins of Philosophy* (3–27).
3   Pyle, *The Ideology of Imagination.*
4   Spivak, 'Megacity' 20.
5   Castells, *The Rise of the Network Society.*

Bibliography

Works by Gayatri Chakravorty Spivak

Books

Myself Must I Remake: The Life and Poetry of W.B. Yeats. New York: Crowell, 1974.
In Other Worlds: Essays in Cultural Politics. New York: Methuen, 1987.
Selected Subaltern Studies. Edited with Ranajit Guha. New York: Oxford University Press, 1988.
The Post-Colonial Critic: Interviews, Strategies, Dialogues. Ed. Sarah Harasym. New York: Routledge, 1990.
Outside in the Teaching Machine. New York: Routledge, 1993.
The Spivak Reader: Selected Works of Gayatri Chakravorty Spivak. Eds Donna Landry and Gerald M. MacLean. New York: Routledge, 1996.
A Critique of Postcolonial Reason: Toward a History of the Vanishing Present. Cambridge, MA: Harvard University Press, 1999.
Imperatives to Re-imagine the Planet / Imperative zur Neuerfindung des Planeten. Ed. Willi Goetschel. Vienna: Passagen, 1999.
Death of a Discipline. New York: Columbia University Press, 2003.
Other Asias. Oxford: Blackwell, forthcoming.
Red Thread. Cambridge, MA: Harvard University Press, forthcoming.
Of Derrida. Oxford: Blackwell, forthcoming.

Translations

Derrida, Jacques. *Of Grammatology.* Baltimore, MA: Johns Hopkins University Press, 1976.
Devi, Mahasweta. *Imaginary Maps.* New York: Routledge, 1995.
—— *Breast Stories.* Calcutta: Seagull, 1997.
—— *Old Women.* Calcutta: Seagull, 1999.
—— *Chotti Munda and His Arrow.* Oxford: Blackwell, 2003.
Mazumdar, Nirode. *Song for Kali: A Cycle of Images and Songs.* Calcutta: Seagull, 2000.

Other cited works by Spivak

'Allégorie et histoire de la poésie: Hypothèse de travail'. Trans. André Jarry. *Poétique* 8 (1971): 427–41.

'American Gender Studies Today'. *Women: A Cultural Review* 10.2 (1999): 217–19.

'Bonding in Difference'. Interview with Alfred Arteaga. *The Spivak Reader*. Eds Donna Landry and Gerald M. MacLean. New York: Routledge, 1996. 15–28.

'The Burden of English'. *Orientalism and the Postcolonial Predicament: Perspectives on South Asia*. Eds Carol A. Breckenridge and Peter van der Veer. Philadelphia, PA: University of Pennsylvania Press, 1993. 134–57.

'Can the Subaltern Speak?' *Marxism and the Interpretation of Culture*. Ed. Cary Nelson and Lawrence Grossberg. Urbana, IL: University of Illinois Press, 1988. 271–313.

'Can the Subaltern Speak? Speculations on Widow-Sacrifice'. *Wedge* 7/8 (1985): 120–30.

'Claiming Transformation: Travel Notes with Pictures'. *Transformations: Thinking through Feminism*. Eds Sara Ahmed et al. London: Routledge, 2000. 119–30.

'Deconstruction and Cultural Studies: Arguments for a Deconstructive Cultural Studies'. *Deconstructions: A User's Guide*. Ed. Nicholas Royle. New York: Palgrave, 2000. 14–43.

'The Denotified and Nomadic Tribes of India: Appeal for Justice and Struggle for Rights'. *Interventions* 1.4 (1999): 590–604.

'A Dialogue on Democracy'. Interview with David Plotke. *Socialist Review* 24.3 (1994): 1–22.

'Diasporas Old and New: Women in the Transnational World'. *Textual Practice* 10.2 (1996): 245–69.

'Displacement and the Discourse of Woman'. *Displacement: Derrida and After*. Ed. Mark Krupnick. Bloomington, IN: Indiana University Press, 1983. 169–95.

'Echo'. *New Literary History* 24.1 (1993): 17–43.

'Ethics and Politics in Tagore, Coetzee, and Certain Scenes of Teaching'. *Diacritics* 32.3–4 (2002): 17–31.

'Feminist Literary Criticism'. *Routledge Encyclopedia of Philosophy*. Ed. Edward Craig. London: Routledge, 1998. 611–14.

'Foreword: Upon Reading the *Companion to Postcolonial Studies*'. *A Companion to Postcolonial Studies*. Eds Henry Schwarz and Sangeeta Ray. Oxford: Blackwell, 2000. xv–xxii.

'Foucault and Najibullah'. *Lyrical Symbols and Narrative Transformations: Essays in Honor of Ralph Freedman*. Eds Kathleen L. Komar and Ross Shideler. Columbia, SC: Camden House, 1998. 218–35.

'French Feminism in an International Frame'. *Yale French Studies* 62 (1981): 154–84.

'From Haverstock Hill Flat to U. S. Classroom, What's Left of Theory?' *What's*

Left of Theory? New Work on the Politics of Literary Theory. Eds. Judith Butler, John Guillory and Kendall Thomas. New York: Routledge, 2000. 1–39.

'Gayatri Spivak on the Politics of the Subaltern'. Interview with Howard Winant. *Socialist Review* 20.3 (1990): 81–97.

'Ghostwriting'. *Diacritics* 25.2 (1995): 65–84.

'*Glas*-Piece: A *compte rendu*'. *Diacritics* 7.3 (1977): 22–43.

'Globalicities: Terror and Its Consequences'. *CR: The New Centennial Review* 4.1 (2004): 73–94.

'How to Read a "Culturally Different" Book'. *Colonial Discourse/Postcolonial Theory.* Eds Francis Barker, Peter Hulme and Margaret Iversen. Manchester: Manchester University Press, 1994. 126–50.

'Il faut s'y prendre en s'en prenant à elles'. *Les fins de l'homme: À partir du travail de Jacques Derrida.* Eds Philippe Lacoue-Labarthe and Jean-Luc Nancy. Paris: Galilée, 1981. 505–15.

'Imperialism and Sexual Difference'. *Oxford Literary Review* 8.1–2 (1986): 225–40.

'Introduction'. *Breast Stories* by Mahasweta Devi. Calcutta: Seagull, 1997. viii–xvi.

'Lives'. *Confessions of the Critics.* Ed. H. Aram Veeser. New York: Routledge, 1996. 205–20.

'Love Me, Love My Ombre, Elle'. *Diacritics* 14.4 (1984): 19–36.

'Megacity'. *Gray Room* 1 (2000): 8–25.

'A Moral Dilemma'. *What Happens to History: The Renewal of Ethics in Contemporary Thought.* Ed. Howard Marchitello. New York: Routledge, 2001. 215–36.

'Moving Devi'. *Cultural Critique* 47 (2001): 120–63.

'Naming Gayatri Spivak'. Interview with Maria Koundoura. *Stanford Humanities Review* 1.1 (1989): 84–97.

'A Note on the New International'. *Parallax* 7.3 [20] (2001): 12–16.

' "On the Cusp of the Personal and the Impersonal": An Interview with Gayatri Chakravorty Spivak.' Interview with Laura E. Lyons and Cynthia Franklin. *Biography* 27.1 (2004): 203–21.

'Other Things Are Never Equal: A Speech'. *Rethinking Marxism* 12.4 (2000): 37–45.

'Our Asias'. *Other Asias.* Oxford: Blackwell, forthcoming.

'The Political Economy of Women as Seen by a Literary Critic'. *Coming to Terms: Feminism, Theory, Politics.* Ed. Elizabeth Weed. New York: Routledge, 1989. 218–29.

'Poststructuralism Meets Schmitt: Schmitt and Poststructuralism: A Response'. *Cardozo Law Review* 21.5–6 (2000): 1723–37.

'Psychoanalysis in Left Field and Fieldworking'. *Speculations after Freud: Psychoanalysis, Philosophy and Culture.* Eds Sonu Shamdasani and Michael Münchow. London: Routledge, 1994. 41–75.

'Questioned on Translation: Adrift'. Interview with Emily Apter. *Public Culture* 13.1 (2001): 13–22.

'The Rani of Sirmur: An Essay in Reading the Archives'. *History and Theory* 24.3 (1985): 247–72.

'Reason and Response'. *Times Higher Education Supplement* 15 October 1999.

'Remembering Derrida'. *Radical Philosophy* 129 (2005): 15–21.

'A Response to "The Difference Within: Feminism and Critical Theory" '. *The Difference Within: Feminism and Critical Theory*. Eds. Elizabeth Meese and Alice Parker. Amsterdam: John Benjamins Publishing Company, 1989. 208–20.

'Responsibility'. *Boundary 2* 21.3 (1994): 19–64.

'Revolutions That As Yet Have No Model: Derrida's *Limited Inc.*' *Diacritics* 10.4 (1980): 29–49.

'Righting Wrongs'. *South Atlantic Quarterly* 103.2–3 (2004): 523–81.

'Setting to Work (Transnational Cultural Studies)'. *A Critical Sense: Interviews with Intellectuals*. Ed. Peter Osborne. London: Routledge, 1996. 162–77.

'Speculation on Reading Marx: After Reading Derrida'. *Post-Structuralism and the Question of History*. Eds Derek Attridge, Robert Young and Geoff Bennington. Cambridge: Cambridge University Press, 1987. 30–62.

'The Staging of Time in *Heremakhonon*'. *Cultural Studies* 17.1 (2003): 85–97.

'Supplementing Marxism'. *Whither Marxism? Global Crises in International Perspective*. Eds Bernd Magnus and Stephen Cullenberg. New York: Routledge, 1995. 109–19.

'Teaching for the Times'. *The Decolonization of the Imagination: Culture, Knowledge and Power*. Eds Jan Niederveen Pieterse and Bhikhu Parekh. London: Zed, 1995. 177–202.

'Terror: A Speech after 9–11'. *Boundary 2* 31.2 (2004): 81–111.

'Thinking About Edward Said: Pages from a Memoir'. *Critical Inquiry* 31.2 (2005): 519–25.

'Thinking Cultural Questions in "Pure" Literary Terms'. *Without Guarantees: In Honour of Stuart Hall*. Ed. Paul Gilroy et al. London: Verso, 2000. 335–57.

'Thoughts on the Principle of Allegory'. *Genre* 5 (1972): 327–52.

'Three Women's Texts and a Critique of Imperialism'. *Critical Inquiry* 12.1 (1985): 243–61.

'Three Women's Texts and *Circumfession*'. *Postcolonialism & Autobiography: Michelle Cliff, David Dabydeen, Opal Palmer Adisa*. Eds Alfred Hornung and Ernstpeter Ruhe. Amsterdam: Rodopi, 1998. 7–22.

'Translating into English'. *Nation, Language, and the Ethics of Translation*. Ed. Sandra Bermann and Michael Wood. Princeton, NJ: Princeton University Press, 2005. 93–110.

'Translation as Culture'. *Parallax* 6.1 (2000): 13–24.

'Translator's Preface'. *Of Grammatology* by Jacques Derrida. Baltimore, MA: Johns Hopkins University Press, 1976. ix–lxxxvii.

'Translator's Preface'. *Imaginary Maps* by Mahasweta Devi. New York: Routledge, 1995. xxiii–xxix.

'Who Claims Alterity?' *Remaking History*. Eds Barbara Kruger and Phil Mariani. Seattle, WA: Bay Press, 1989. 269–92.

Cited works by other authors

Al-Kassim, Dina. 'The Face of Foreclosure'. *Interventions* 4.2 (2002): 168–75.

Amin, Shahid. 'Gandhi as Mahatma'. *Selected Subaltern Studies*. Eds Gayatri Chakravorty Spivak and Ranajit Guha. New York: Oxford University Press, 1988. 288–348.

Apter, Emily. 'Afterlife of a Discipline'. *Comparative Literature* 57.3 (2005): 201–6.

Arnott, Jill. 'French Feminism in a South African Frame? Gayatri Spivak and the Problem of Representation in South African Feminism'. *South African Feminisms: Writing, Theory, and Criticism, 1990–1994*. Ed. M.J. Daymond. New York: Garland, 1996. 77–89.

Attridge, Derek. *The Singularity of Literature*. London: Routledge, 2004.

Bal, Mieke. 'Three-Way Misreading'. *Diacritics* 30.1 (2000): 2–24.

Baucom, Ian. 'Cryptic, Withheld, Singular'. *Nepantla* 1.2 (2000): 413–29.

Benjamin, Walter. 'The Task of the Translator'. Trans. Harry Zohn. *Selected Writings*. Eds Marcus Bullock and Michael W. Jennings. Vol. 1. Cambridge, MA: Harvard University Press, 1996. 253–63.

Bhabha, Homi K. *The Location of Culture*. London: Routledge, 1994.

Castells, Manuel. *The Rise of the Network Society*. 2nd edn. Oxford: Blackwell, 2000.

Chomsky, Noam. *9–11*. New York: Seven Stories, 2002.

Cummings, Sara, Henk Van Dam and Minke Valk, eds. *Gender Training: The Source Book*. Amsterdam/Oxford: Royal Tropical Institute/Oxfam, 1998.

Damrosch, David. *What Is World Literature?* Princeton, NJ: Princeton University Press, 2003.

de Man, Paul. *Allegories of Reading: Figural Language in Rousseau, Nietzsche, Rilke, and Proust*. New Haven, CT: Yale University Press, 1979.

Derrida, Jacques. 'Autoimmunity: Real and Symbolic Suicides: A Dialogue with Jacques Derrida'. Trans. Pascale-Anne Brault and Michael Naas. *Philosophy in a Time of Terror: Dialogues with Jürgen Habermas and Jacques Derrida*. Ed. Giovanna Borradori. Chicago: University of Chicago Press, 2003. 85–136.

——— *The Gift of Death*. Trans. David Wills. Chicago: University of Chicago Press, 1995.

——— *Given Time: I. Counterfeit Money*. Trans. Peggy Kamuf. Chicago: University of Chicago Press, 1992.

——— *Margins of Philosophy*. Trans. Alan Bass. Brighton: Harvester Press, 1982.

——— 'Marx & Sons'. Trans. G.M. Goshgarian. *Ghostly Demarcations: A Symposium on Jacques Derrida's* Specters of Marx. Ed. Michael Sprinker. London: Verso, 1999. 213–69.

——— 'Psyche: Inventions of the Other'. Trans. Catherine Porter. *Reading De Man*

Reading. Eds Lindsay Waters and Wlad Godzich. Minneapolis, MN: University of Minnesota Press, 1989. 25–65.

—— *Rogues: Two Essays on Reason*. Trans. Pascale-Anne Brault and Michael Naas. Stanford, CA: Stanford University Press, 2005.

—— 'Shibboleth: For Paul Celan'. Trans. Joshua Wilner. *Acts of Literature*. Ed. Derek Attridge. New York: Routledge, 1992. 370–413.

—— 'Signature Event Context'. Trans. Alan Bass. *Margins of Philosophy*. Brighton: Harvester Press, 1982. 307–30.

—— *Specters of Marx: The State of the Debt, the Work of Mourning, and the New International*. Trans. Peggy Kamuf. New York: Routledge, 1994.

—— *The Truth in Painting*. Trans. Geoff Bennington and Ian McLeod. Chicago: University of Chicago Press, 1987.

—— *Writing and Difference*. Trans. Alan Bass. Chicago: University of Chicago Press, 1978.

Derrida, Jacques and Anne Dufourmantelle. *Of Hospitality*. Trans. Rachel Bowlby. Stanford, CA: Stanford University Press, 2000.

Descartes, René. *Discourse on Method and the Meditations*. Trans. F.E. Sutcliffe. Harmondsworth: Penguin, 1968.

Devi, Mahasweta. ' "Telling History": Gayatri Chakravorty Spivak Interviews Mahasweta Devi'. *Chotti Munda and His Arrow*. Trans. Gayatri Chakravorty Spivak. Oxford: Blackwell, 2003. ix–xxiii.

Dirlik, Arif. 'The Postcolonial Aura: Third World Criticism in the Age of Global Capitalism'. *Critical Inquiry* 20.2 (1994): 328–56.

Eagleton, Terry. 'In the Gaudy Supermarket'. *London Review of Books* 13 May 1999: 3, 5–6.

Fanon, Frantz. *Black Skin, White Masks*. Trans. Charles Lam Markmann. London: Pluto Press, 1986.

Foucault, Michel. *Language, Counter-Memory, Practice: Selected Essays and Interviews*. Trans. Donald F. Bouchard and Sherry Simon. Ed. Donald F. Bouchard. Ithaca, NY: Cornell University Press, 1977.

—— 'What Is Critique?' *What Is Enlightenment? Eighteenth-Century Answers and Twentieth-Century Questions*. Ed. James Schmidt. Berkeley, CA: University of California Press, 1996. 382–98.

Freud, Sigmund. ' "A Child Is Being Beaten" (A Contribution to the Study of the Origin of Sexual Perversions)'. 1919. Trans. Alix Strachey and James Strachey. *The Standard Edition of the Complete Psychological Works of Sigmund Freud*. London: Hogarth Press and the Institute of Psycho-Analysis, 1953–. 17: 175–204.

——'Thoughts for the Times on War and Death'. 1915. Trans. E.C. Mayne. *Standard Edition*. 14: 275–300.

Gallop, Jane. 'The Translation of Deconstruction'. *Qui Parle* 8.1 (1994): 45–62.

Guha, Ranajit. 'On Some Aspects of the Historiography of Colonial India'. *Selected Subaltern Studies*. Eds. Gayatri Chakravorty Spivak and Ranajit Guha. New York: Oxford University Press, 1988. 37–44.

Hallward, Peter. *Absolutely Postcolonial: Writing Between the Singular and the Specific*. Manchester: Manchester University Press, 2001.

Hamacher, Werner. 'Lectio: Paul De Man's Imperative'. Trans. Susan Bernstein. *Reading De Man Reading*. Eds Lindsay Waters and Wlad Godzich. Minneapolis, MN: University of Minnesota Press, 1989. 171–201.

Harvey, David. *The New Imperialism*. Oxford: Oxford University Press, 2003.

Homer, Sean. 'A Short History of the MLG'. 1996. Online: <http://mlg. eserver.org/about/history.html>. Accessed 26 June 2005.

Jameson, Fredric. *The Political Unconscious: Narrative as a Socially Symbolic Act*. Ithaca, NY: Cornell University Press, 1981.

Keats, John. *The Letters of John Keats*. Ed. Hyder Edward Rollins. Vol. 2. Cambridge, MA: Harvard University Press, 1952.

Keenan, Thomas. *Fables of Responsibility: Aberrations and Predicaments in Ethics and Politics*. Stanford, CA: Stanford University Press, 1997.

Klein, Melanie. 'Love, Guilt and Reparation'. 1937. *Love, Guilt and Reparation and Other Works 1921–1945*. London: Vintage, 1998. 306–43.

—— *The Psycho-Analysis of Children*. 1932. Trans. Alix Strachey and H.A. Thorner. Revised edn. London: Vintage, 1997.

Lacoue-Labarthe, Philippe, and Jean-Luc Nancy, eds. *Les fins de l'homme: À partir du travail de Jacques Derrida*. Paris: Galilée, 1981.

Levinas, Emmanuel. *Otherwise Than Being, or, Beyond Essence*. 1974. Trans. Alphonso Lingis. Pittsburgh, PA: Duquesne University Press, 1998.

Macaulay, Thomas Babington. 'Thomas Babington Macaulay on Education for India'. *Imperialism*. Ed. Philip D. Curtin. New York: Walker and Company, 1971. 178–91.

Mamdani, Mahmood. *Citizen and Subject: Contemporary Africa and the Legacy of Late Colonialism*. Princeton, NJ: Princeton University Press, 1996.

Marx, Karl. *Capital: A Critique of Political Economy*. Trans. Ben Fowkes. Vol. 1. New York: Vintage, 1977.

—— *Capital: A Critique of Political Economy*. Trans. David Fernbach. Vol. 3. Harmondsworth: Penguin, 1981.

—— *The Eighteenth Brumaire of Louis Bonaparte*. 1852. Trans. Ben Fowkes. *Surveys from Exile: Political Writings: Volume 2*. Ed. David Fernbach. Harmondsworth: Penguin, 1973. 143–249.

—— *Grundrisse: Foundations of the Critique of Political Economy*. Trans. Martin Nicolaus. New York: Vintage, 1973.

McEwan, Ian. *Saturday*. London: Jonathan Cape, 2005.

Medovoi, Leerom, Shankar Raman and Benjamin Robinson. 'Can the Sub-altern Vote?' *Socialist Review* 20.3 (1990): 133–49.

Mies, Maria. *Patriarchy and Accumulation on a World Scale: Women in the International Division of Labour*. 2nd edn. London: Zed Books, 1998.

Miller, J. Hillis. *The Ethics of Reading: Kant, De Man, Eliot, Trollope, James, and Benjamin*. New York: Columbia University Press, 1987.

Moore-Gilbert, Bart. *Postcolonial Theory: Contexts, Practices, Politics*. London: Verso, 1997.

Moretti, Franco. 'Conjectures on World Literature'. *Debating World Literature*. Ed. Christopher Prendergast. London: Verso, 2004. 148–62.

Morton, Stephen. *Gayatri Chakravorty Spivak*. London: Routledge, 2003.

Ngũgĩ wa Thiong'o. *Decolonising the Mind: The Politics of Language in African Literature*. London: James Currey, 1986.

—— *Detained: A Writer's Prison Diary*. London: Heinemann, 1981.

Nkrumah, Kwame. *Consciencism: Philosophy and Ideology for De-Colonization*. Revised edn. New York: Monthly Review Press, 1970.

Paglia, Camille et al. 'American Gender Studies Today'. *Women: A Cultural Review* 10.2 (1999): 213–19.

Parry, Benita. 'Problems in Current Theories of Colonial Discourse'. *Oxford Literary Review* 9.1–2 (1987): 27–58.

Plato. *Apology*. Trans. Benjamin Jowett. *The Dialogues of Plato*. Vol. 1. New York: Random House, 1937. 401–23.

Pyle, Forest. *The Ideology of Imagination: Subject and Society in the Discourse of Romanticism*. Stanford, CA: Stanford University Press, 1995.

Ryan, Michael. *Marxism and Deconstruction: A Critical Articulation*. Baltimore, MA: Johns Hopkins University Press, 1982.

Said, Edward W. *Orientalism*. New York: Pantheon Books, 1978.

Shelley, Percy Bysshe. 'A Defence of Poetry; or Remarks Suggested by an Essay Entitled "The Four Ages of Poetry" '. *Shelley's Poetry and Prose*. Eds Donald Reiman and Sharon B. Powers. New York: Norton, 1977. 480–508.

Shetty, Sandhya, and Elizabeth Jane Bellamy. 'Postcolonialism's Archive Fever'. *Diacritics* 30.1 (2000): 25–48.

Shiva, Vandana. *Biopiracy: The Plunder of Nature and Knowledge*. Boston, MA: South End Press, 1997.

—— *Stolen Harvest: The Hijacking of the Global Food Supply*. Cambridge, MA: South End Press, 2000.

Shumway, David R. 'The Star System in Literary Studies'. *PMLA* 112.1 (1997): 85–100.

Sprinker, Michael, ed. *Ghostly Demarcations: A Symposium on Jacques Derrida's Specters of Marx*. London: Verso, 1999.

Varadharajan, Asha. *Exotic Parodies: Subjectivity in Adorno, Said, and Spivak*. Minneapolis, MN: University of Minnesota Press, 1995.

Young, Robert. Review of *Outside in the Teaching Machine* by Gayatri Chakravorty Spivak. *Textual Practice* 10.1 (1996): 228–38.

—— *White Mythologies: Writing History and the West*. London: Routledge, 1990.

Index